Silent Nights

Dr Pat Spungin

PRENTICE HALL LIFE

If life is what you make it, then making it better starts here.

What we learn today can change our lives tomorrow. It can change our goals or change our minds; open up new opportunities or simply inspire us to make a difference. That's why we have created a new breed of books that do more to help you make more of your life.

Whether you want more confidence or less stress, a new skill or a different perspective, we've designed *Prentice Hall Life* books to help you to make a change for the better. Together with our authors we share a commitment to bring you the brightest ideas and best ways to manage your life, work and wealth.

In these pages we hope you'll find the ideas you need for the life *you* want.

Go on, help yourself.

It's what you make it

Silent Nights

How to develop a peaceful
sleeping routine

Dr Pat Spungin

PEARSON
Prentice Hall
LIFE

Pearson Education Limited
Edinburgh Gate
Harlow
Essex CM20 2JE
England

ISBN: 978-0-273-71479-8
Commissioning Editor: Emma Shackleton
Project Editor: Helena Caldon
Designer: Annette Peppis
Cover Design: R&D&Co
Production Controller: Franco Forgione

Printed and bound by Henry Ling, UK

The Publisher's policy is to use paper manufactured from sustainable forests.

Contents

1 The importance of sleep 7

2 And so to bed 39

3 Getting into a sleep routine 65

4 I don't want to go to bed! 89

5 Waking in the night 117

6 Other sleep problems 149

7 Early risers 173

8 10 steps to better sleep 197

Resources 221

The importance of sleep

As the founder of the parenting website raisingkids. co.uk., I am often asked for advice on a variety of issues to do with looking after children. Of all the questions that we receive from parents or carers on the website, an overwhelming number are about their child's sleeping habits. From how and when to establish a good routine for a baby, all the way through to how to get a teenager out of bed before mid-afternoon at the weekend, managing a child's sleep seems to be a common and recurrent concern amongst parents.

How common are sleep problems?

If you have a child with a sleep problem it might bring you some consolation to know that you are not alone. Research suggests that 20 per cent of under-twos and 5 per cent of five-year-olds regularly wake in the night; whereas 22 per cent of nine-month-olds, 15 to 20 per cent of toddlers aged between one and two, and 16 per cent of children aged three and above will have difficulty settling themselves to sleep on their own.

And, frustratingly, it doesn't always seem to get better when they go to school: a recent study reported that 37 per cent of school-age children experience significant sleep problems, including a reluctance to go to sleep, waking up in the middle of the night, suffering nightmares and also sleepwalking.

Children with physical and mental handicaps in particular are likely to have issues with sleeping, and indeed it is estimated that 67 per cent of learning-disabled children will experience sleep-related problems.

What are the effects of sleep deprivation?

Both adults and children in our society live very busy lives. To be able to cope with the stresses and strains of everyday living we need to have replenishing sleep. For adults that amounts to 7–8 hours' unbroken sleep per night, and for children it is between 16 and 9 hours, depending on their age. Unfortunately, a significant number of adults sleep less than this and so do many children. Sleep deprivation has serious consequences for both adults and children.

For children

For a growing child, good sleep habits are as important as good eating habits. A good night's sleep nourishes the brain and helps the body to grow. Most parents are concerned about their child getting the sleep he requires. They know that without sufficient sleep their baby or child may be grumpy and lethargic the following day.

This tiredness will manifest itself in different ways: babies who don't get enough sleep are more emotional, fuss more and will often spend much of the late afternoon and evening crying. Children of school age who are chronically sleep-deprived will find themselves unable to concentrate in class, which in turn has a detrimental effect on their educational progress.

In fact, there is growing evidence that this is a much larger problem than you would think. There are many children who are significantly sleep-deprived. Both poor-quality sleep and not enough of it will have an impact on several aspects of a child's development:

Behaviour

Recent US research has revealed that two- and three-year-old children who were sleeping less than 10 hours in a 24-hour period were at greatest risk of exhibiting problems such as oppositional or non-compliant behaviour, 'acting out' behaviours and aggression. Infants who slept up to three hours less than the average for their age tended to be more irritable, harder to handle and more prone to crying than their more settled and placid contemporaries.

Learning and cognitive development

A good nap may not only keep babies from getting cranky, it also helps them to learn various skills and to absorb certain information. A new study suggests that napping plays an important role in this ability, by allowing a child time to process and retain the information he's exposed to while he is awake.

Other research, involving babies of five months old, shows that naps are important for the development of their persistence and attention span – key elements in a baby's ability to learn. This research concludes that a child who gets enough sleep, without interruption, should wake up and find himself in a state of 'optimal wakefulness', ready to interact with the world.

So for the child's sake as much as for the parents', it is important for parents to find out as much information as they can about what constitutes a good night's sleep, how to know if their child is getting as much sleep as he needs, what to expect at different ages and how to react when he is constantly disturbing the household with nightly forays into the parental bed.

For parents

Most parents know that they have signed up for a period of sleepless nights while their baby is very young and still feeding in the night. They expect to be disturbed when their child is unwell or teething. They are also aware that the occasional significant change in their household may unsettle their child and cause the occasional sleep problem. All of this is to be expected; however, what most parents find difficult to cope with is night after night of broken sleep, with no end in sight!

Parents whose sleep is constantly disrupted still have to get up in the morning and either go to work or care for their family and household. Working parents are expected to be bright-eyed and bushy-tailed on a limited amount of sleep, but their work will undoubtedly suffer if they are below par. They might also find themselves being more irritable with colleagues, staff and customers during the long working day.

For parents with a busy household to take care of, as well as other children, the daily routine is seriously affected by the disruption caused by broken sleep. At-home parents are advised to catch up on their missed sleep while their baby is napping. This sounds like a sensible idea in theory, but in reality this is not always possible – particularly if there are other children at home all day too. However, if the baby is the only child at home, once he is in the routine of predictable sleep – for example, one or two naps in the day – these times are golden opportunities for parents to get on with other jobs or just to take five minutes out from the demands of the family.

Keeping everyone up

Remember, babies crying or toddlers calling out or wandering around in the night will disturb the sleep not only of the adults in the family, but also of the other children. Although most older children – like many husbands – will sleep through night-time disturbances, it is worth checking that their sleep is not disturbed, especially if they have school the next day.

Whether away at work or at home with the children, parents who are tense and sleep-deprived unknowingly communicate their anxiety about sleep to their child. Their own lack of sleep means that they are less able to deal with their child's sleep problems. And so the cycle begins...

The importance of sleep for body and mind

Sleep is essential for all living creatures, and sleep is especially important for children because it has a direct impact on both their mental and physical development.

In the brain there are sleep centres which control sleep activity: while the body sleeps, the brain continues to work. One of its functions, particularly in childhood and adolescence, is to secrete a growth hormone from the pituitary gland that is essential for physical development.

Our circadian rhythms, or, more simply, our sleep–wake cycle, are regulated by light and dark. These rhythms take time to develop. They are not there at birth, as can be seen in the irregular sleeping patterns of the newborn baby. In the first few weeks after birth a baby may experience day–night confusion; the baby will often be very sleepy during the day and very wakeful at night. This is not unusual. However, by six weeks these circadian rhythms are beginning to develop and by six months most infants have a predictable sleep–wake cycle that coincides, in large part, with periods of light and dark.

The stages of sleep

When we sleep our body goes through five different stages within a sleep cycle. Although there are five distinct stages in a sleep cycle, each one characterized by different types of brain waves and a differing degree of physical arousal, the main differences are between REM (rapid eye movement) sleep and non-REM sleep.

Rapid eye movement (REM)

This is the period of light or active sleep when there is rapid movement of the eyes, which is visible beneath the eyelids. During REM sleep, our brain is active and so this is the stage when dreaming is most likely to occur. Our body becomes immobile, breathing and heart rates are irregular, eyes jerk rapidly and limb muscles are temporarily paralyzed.

REM sleep occurs every 90–100 minutes in adults. Infants have shorter cycles, lasting between 50 and 60 minutes, and spend almost 50 per cent of their sleep time in REM sleep. In premature babies REM sleep accounts for four-fifths of total sleep time. Over time, the amount of REM sleep decreases, falling to 30 per cent as the child reaches six months old. From three years onwards, the amount of REM sleep is the same as adults', at 20 per cent.

Non-rapid eye movement (NREM)

This is the period of deep or 'quiet' sleep. During NREM sleep, blood supply to the muscles is increased, energy is restored, tissue growth and repair occur and important hormones are released for growth and development. In this deep sleep there is no eye movement or muscle activity and it is very difficult to wake the sleeper. Some children might experience bedwetting, sleepwalking or night terrors during this phase.

Moving from the deep NREM sleep to the lighter, more active REM sleep involves a degree of arousal – the sleeper is not fully awake during this period, but he will also no longer be in deep sleep. At this stage the sleeper may stir, babies may whimper or cry out and adults might rearrange their bedding and change position. All sleepers experience these periods of partial waking and most return to sleep without fully waking.

A child completes a sleep cycle every hour or so and experiences vulnerable periods for night-waking within that period. Waking in the night is therefore normal and to be expected. The key thing to remember is that it is also normal for the child to return to sleep without any intervention.

Benefits of REM sleep for babies

Sleep researchers believe that babies sleep 'smarter' than adults do. During REM sleep the brain is active, with blood flow to the brain nearly doubling. This increased blood flow is particularly evident in the area of the brain that automatically controls breathing. During REM sleep the body increases its manufacture of certain nerve proteins, the building blocks of the brain.

In their first two years, babies' brains grow to nearly 70 per cent of adult volume, and it is believed that during this stage of rapid growth the brain needs to continue functioning while the babies sleep in order to develop properly.

It is interesting to note that premature babies spend even more of their sleep time (approximately 90 per cent) in REM sleep, and this could be to accelerate their brain growth. It therefore seems clear that having good-quality sleep is critically important for an infant's cognitive development.

How sleeping patterns change throughout childhood

As the baby's brain matures, the patterns and rhythms of sleep change under the influence of biological forces that are responsive to the light–dark cycle. This mechanism automatically tries to ensure that the body is sleeping at the correct time and that the timings and amounts of the various stages and types of sleep are correct.

Parents who are trying to help their child learn good sleep habits need to be attentive to these changes as their child develops. For parents, developing a good sleep routine with their child means synchronizing natural biological tendencies with the day–night routines of the household.

There are five points of change in an average child's sleeping habits, although not all children will conform to this pattern. So the most helpful advice here is that you should try to be sensitive to your baby's individual needs.

1 Many parents notice a remarkable change in their baby when he reaches around six weeks old. This is when a baby who had previously been sleeping at all times of the day and night will begin to sleep longer at night, usually for about five hours at a stretch.

2 At between 12 and 16 weeks, daytime sleep starts to fall into a regular pattern involving two, sometimes three, naps, followed by increasing amount of night sleep.

3 By nine months night feeding is over (often earlier) and the third nap disappears.

4 Some time in the second year, the infant gives up the morning nap.

5 By around 2½ –3½ years old an infant will have dropped his regular afternoon nap completely.

Babies and newborns

Newborns tend to sleep for a total of 10.5 to 18 hours a day on an irregular schedule, with periods of one to three hours spent awake. Their longest sleep cycle is only four to five hours, and the amount the baby sleeps ranges from a few minutes to a couple of hours. During sleep babies are often active – twitching their arms and legs, smiling, sucking and generally appearing restless, which is behaviour typical of REM sleep. From birth onwards, sleep amounts slowly decrease and baby is awake more often.

Between the ages of two and six weeks, some babies go through a period of fussiness and increasingly alert behaviour. This is due to their developing nervous system causing excessive arousal, a phase which passes as the child matures.

Newborns express their need to sleep in different ways: some fuss, cry, rub their eyes or indicate their readiness for bed with individual gestures. It helps babies to develop good sleep habits if you put them to bed when they are drowsy, but not asleep. If they learn to fall asleep in their cot without the crutches of someone rocking, soothing, cuddling them and so on, they will eventually learn to associate being put into their cot with falling asleep and will be able to settle themselves when they are put down.

When infants are put to bed drowsy but not asleep, they are more likely to become 'self-soothers', which means that when they have periods of arousal during the night they are able to settle themselves back to sleep. Babies who have got used to falling asleep with parental help will cry out for their parents during the night because they need them in order to be able to get back to sleep.

In the very beginning, newborn infants are relatively unaffected by their environment and can fall asleep surrounded by high levels of noise, although a sudden startling noise might wake them. At this stage the advice for parents is to follow your child's sleeping pattern and not try to 'shape' it as yet, because (as mentioned on page 17) at around six weeks parents will begin to see a natural change in their habits.

Three to eleven months

From the age of three months to the end of the first year, babies will sleep, on average, for a total of around 14.5 hours (including both night-time and daytime sleep), although 10 per cent of children will sleep less than 11 hours, and a similar number more than 16 hours.

By three months, daytime sleep has begun to regularize. Don't worry if your child doesn't conform to the average: as long as you are sensitive to his personal sleep needs you can make sure that he is getting enough sleep. If you are worried that that he isn't getting enough sleep, look for signs such as falling asleep when not in his cot, irritability and fretfulness, and treat this as a cue to increase his sleep time or add in a nap. Babies quickly move from being drowsy and tired to being over-tired, so it is important for you to watch for signs that he is ready to sleep and act on them as they appear.

When their baby is aged between about four and six months, many parents begin to offer him solids on the assumption that solid food will help the baby sleep longer. However, there is no evidence that food has this effect. Much more likely is that between three and four months the baby's brain begins to produce the hormone melatonin, which induces drowsiness and relaxes the muscles surrounding the gut. Mothers of colicky babies who have been crying for two or three hours every evening will find that at three months the crying suddenly stops.

Attachment and separation anxiety

At around eight or nine months old a baby will become attached to his principal caregiver, which is usually his mother. Along with this process of intense bonding with the mother comes the fear of separation from her. This is the time when babies who have previously settled well at night may now cry as their mother leaves the room.

By six months of age, night-time feedings are usually no longer necessary and many infants will be sleeping through the night, and certainly 70–80 per cent will do so by nine months of age.

Infants typically sleep for between 9 and 12 hours during the night and take 30-minute to two-hour naps, one to three times a day – fewer as they reach age one. At six months the majority of infants sleep 2.5 to 4 hours per day during the day, with 15 per cent sleeping for more than four hours and five per cent for less than 2.5 hours. Although it is possible to make a sleepy baby wakeful, it is not possible to make a baby sleep. Around the end of the first year the infant gives up the morning nap and may then sleep a little longer during the afternoon nap.

In the first year, a baby's pattern of sleeping and wakefulness appears to be, to a large extent, biologically controlled. Babies differ in how long they nap and it seems to be something that is innate: you cannot make a short napper into a longer napper. According to research, having an afternoon nap does not affect the amount of sleep at night, so don't keep your baby up late in the hope that he will sleep later into the morning; he will only become irritable and over-tired and then find it difficult to settle. A study of infants showed that both the regular nappers and the non-nappers slept for 10.5 hours a night when three years old; it was just that the napper was having an extra hour or two of sleep during the day.

A word about naps

In the first year most babies will have two naps per day. There is evidence that a baby's nap differs from night-time sleep and that the morning nap also differs from the afternoon nap: there appears to be more REM sleep in the morning nap than in the afternoon, and more REM sleep during the night. Since REM sleep is associated with the development of the brain in early life, it is important to make sure that babies are not simply getting enough sleep, but are also sleeping at the right time. In the second year most babies give up their morning nap, with around 17 per cent of children taking just one nap per day by their first birthday.

Toddlers

In general, toddlers need about 12 to 14 hours' sleep in a 24-hour period. By about 18 months of age most toddlers will have only one nap in the afternoon, lasting about one to three hours. It is a good idea to avoid napping too close to bedtime, as it may mean the child then is not ready to go to sleep at night until later than usual.

By their first birthday many children will already be in a settled and predictable routine. Developmental issues may put paid to all that. Some toddlers may now become more unpredictable in their sleeping habits as they grow more assertive and more likely to make a fuss if bedtime doesn't go according to their liking. Children of this age have a great curiosity about the world and are reluctant to give up the excitement of discovery and play for bed – especially if that play is with a beloved parent who may have been out at work all day.

For a parent, this is the stage when it may become more difficult to recognize the signals for sleep. A toddler will quickly become over-tired from just being tired. He may seem wide awake, intensely involved in everything that is going on around him and full of energy, but then he will suddenly appear exhausted, but fight it, and then become over-tired, fretful, prone to tears and tantrums and, para-doxically, too tired to sleep.

If you are not sure if your child is getting enough sleep, keep an eye out for any daytime sleepiness and behaviour problems, as these may signal that he is getting poor sleep or has a sleep problem.

Many developmental changes occur during a child's second and third years. The tractable baby becomes an independent and forceful toddler, full of energy to explore the world. Many factors can interfere with a child's sleep: his drive for independence and an increase in his motor, cognitive and social abilities; his ability to get out of bed; separation anxiety; the need for autonomy and the development of his imagination. As a result of all this change, during the toddler years many children experience sleep problems, including resisting going to bed and night-time awakening. Night fears and nightmares are also common at this age.

Pre-school children

Pre-schoolers typically sleep for between 11 and 13 hours each night and most do not nap during the day after five years of age – even on an irregular basis. With luck they will now be into a good bedtime routine and settle quickly and easily most nights. Almost all children will have moved from a cot to a bed. They are now mobile and able to get out of bed as and when they wish! I don't have to spell out the implications of this for going to bed, waking (maybe several times) during the night or early-morning waking.

This is a period when fears and fantasies may affect their sleep. As their imagination flourishes, pre-schoolers will commonly experience night-time fears and nightmares, and in addition sleepwalking and sleep terrors peak during pre-school years. Some children will develop a fear of the dark, others become scared of monsters or burglars and resist going to bed. Most children will have grown out of these fears by the time they start school. It's important help them deal with their fears so that they can stick with their bedtime routine. In Chapter 5 we outline some simple ways in which you can do this.

During the pre-school years many children first attend nursery school. For some children this move away from the safety and security of the family can have an adverse effect on their sleeping habits. They may fear being left in the evening and come downstairs repeatedly. If they wake in the night, they may start coming to their parents' bed for comfort and reassurance.

Many pre-schoolers will experience the birth of a new sibling, the return to work of their mother, moving house, the death of a close relative and possibly family breakdown. Children are unsettled by any such changes in their world and the results will often be sleepless nights and bedtime resistance. This is perfectly normal and the best thing for parents to do is be flexible about bedtime routine and give the reassurance their child is seeking.

Sleep and school-age children (5–12 years)

Children between the ages of five and 12 need 10–11 hours of sleep, not least because they will be experiencing an increasing demand on their time and energy resources as a result of being at school – from things such as homework, sports and other extra-curricular and social activities.

Many schoolchildren live in a screen-dominated environment, with easy access to televisions, DVD players, games consoles and computers. A very high percentage of seven year olds in the UK have a television in their bedroom, contrary to the advice of sleep experts. This recommendation comes because it has been revealed that watching television close to bedtime has been associated with bedtime resistance, difficulty falling asleep, anxiety around sleep and sleeping for fewer hours.

At school children often face new issues such as teasing, bullying, worries about their achievement in class or friendships. Many children are reluctant to talk to their parents about these things and their pent-up anxieties will frequently come out at night. Research suggests that 37 per cent of children are suffering from some form of sleep issue and resulting sleep deprivation. Poor or inadequate sleep can lead to mood swings, behavioural problems (such as hyperactivity) and cognitive difficulties which will have an impact on a child's ability to learn in school.

Typical sleep patterns amongst children under

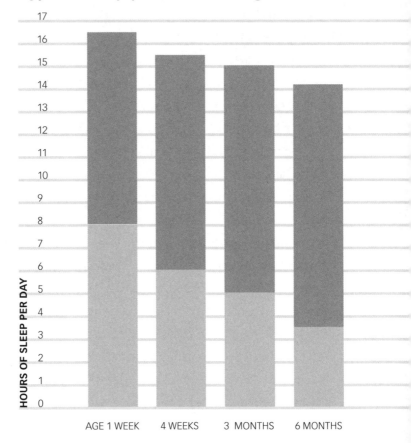

How much sleep does my child need?

Remember that the amount of sleep each child needs is individual. As a rough guide, use the charts below and on pages 28–9 to see if your child is getting enough sleep. If he sleeps more or less than the norm, trust your parental instinct before deciding there is a problem.

■ NIGHT ■ DAY

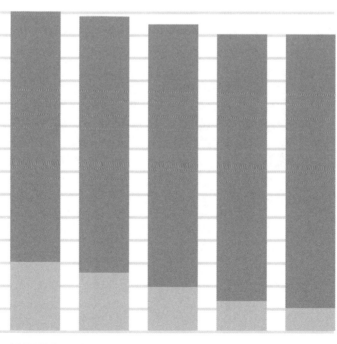

9 MONTHS   12 MONTHS   18 MONTHS   2 YEARS   3 YEARS

On the preceding pages is a diagram which sets out the average amount of sleep required by a pre-school child, at different ages up to the age of four.

The chart below goes on to show the amount of sleep required by children from the age of four years and up to the age of 18.

How can I tell if my child is getting enough sleep?

If you are not sure if your child is getting enough sleep, there are a few signs you can look out for which will help you decide.

Typical sleep patterns – school-age children

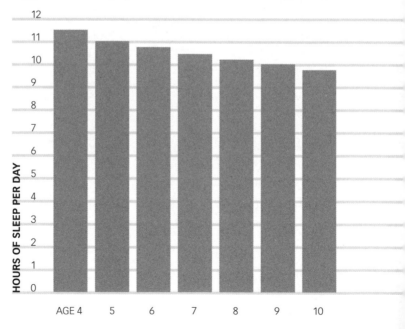

Babies

On the whole, babies will take the sleep they need as and when they need it. As they get older there are things that may disturb their sleep, such as teething or being cold, but most very small babies are able to fall asleep when they are tired unless there is something that disturbs them, such as repeated loud noises.

If a baby is kept up when tired he may become fussy and fretful and start to cry inconsolably. A natural response by the parents is to try to soothe him by rocking him, attempting to get him to smile, or walking up and down with him in their arms. All these actions will overstimulate the

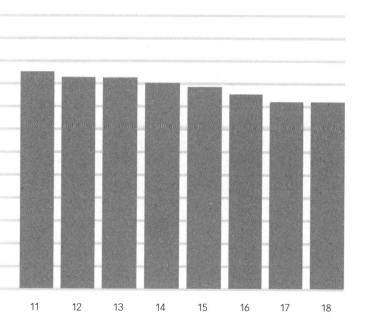

baby. The best thing to do is to put him down in his cot and leave him for a few minutes. Wait for him to settle (stay in the room if you wish) and pretty soon you will find that he falls asleep.

Toddlers

As toddlers get older they become more interested in things around them and they will be reluctant to stop what they are doing in order to go to bed. After all, the world is now far too interesting to stop looking, listening and learning and for it to be given up for the peace and quiet of the bedroom!

If you find that you have to wake your toddler in the morning, or if he is falling asleep in places other than his bed (for example, while watching television), or if he gets 'hyper', fractious or irritable, chances are he isn't getting enough sleep.

Primary-school children

Primary-school children have to be up in the morning in time for school, and the ultimate test of whether or not your child is getting enough sleep is if he is difficult to wake in the morning and slow to get moving.

Is he bad-tempered in the morning? If he goes to school by car, does he always fall asleep on the journey? Does his teacher ever say that he is slow, grumpy or lethargic in lessons, or does she think that his schoolwork is not as good as it could be? All these behaviours signal that he may not be getting the sleep he needs.

How parents benefit from their child's good sleep habits

Aside from solving your own issues of sleep deprivation and improving both your child's and your quality of daily life, encouraging your child into good sleep habits can have additional benefits and solve other, less obviously important problems that arise for parents.

Children have the ability that, once they decide to go to sleep they just do it; adults have more complicated attitudes to sleep. Parents who have their own sleep issues may find that one disturbance extends far beyond the amount of time the child is awake. A 20-minute waking period for a baby or toddler can become a two-hour period of sleeplessness for his mother or father.

For parents, there is also another advantage of getting their children into a good sleep routine: it allows them to have some adult time. If the children are asleep in bed for the night at a reasonable hour, parents can enjoy a meal and a chat together, watch television or go out and leave their children with a babysitter secure in the knowledge that the children will not wake up. During the first few months of having a baby, in particular, it is vital that parents create some time for themselves in order to maintain their relationship and see how it will work in their new, very different way of life.

Similarly, if an older child is up and down all evening, comes into the parents' bed during the night or cannot sleep except in the parents' bed, all these have an effect on the relationship between the parents. Many couples experience a type of estrangement after the birth of their first, or even subsequent, child. Dads can feel excluded from the tight-knit relationship mothers establish with the newborn infant; mothers are also tired and emotional and busy caring for and feeding the baby, which often doesn't

How routine can help sleep

Not all babies are the same: from birth some children are temperamentally more easily disturbed and more fretful, cry more and sleep less. These babies are also less able to 'self-soothe' and need more help to establish a good sleep pattern. A structured routine of sleeping, eating, bathtime and so on all contribute to a sense of solidity and calm in a child's life, which is very important to his psychological wellbeing. Research has also confirmed that children who are brought up in households that have a sense of order and stability tend to grow up with a strong sense of security themselves.

When a mother finds herself struggling with a new baby when she has previously had a very 'easy' baby, she may believe that she is doing something wrong or different from before. She isn't; he's just a different baby with different needs. It can take longer and be less easy to get some 'difficult' babies into a regular sleeping schedule.

leave enough time to attend to the needs of their partner. If sleep deprivation is fed into the mix, fatigue, lack of adult time and irritability with one another can all make it even more difficult for parents to recreate the affection that brought them together in the first place.

What applics to an evening spent together enjoying each other's company is even more true when it comes to making

but it is precisely those babies who benefit most from a good routine which takes into account their temperamental sensitivities.

Sleep manuals are available that imply that, with the 'right' approach, all children can be trained to sleep according to the clock. Indeed, some children may adapt to the requirements of the suggested routine very easily, and mothers whose children are sleeping like clockwork as a result of applying these rigid rules will naturally believe that because it worked for them it can work for anyone. Not so: it is more likely that the routine worked because they had the kind of baby who was able to fit easily and with a limited amount of distress into the prescribed schedule. It might be more beneficial for mothers who have babies who are difficult to settle to wait until their child has matured a little before trying to fit him into someone else's routine.

sure that the marital bed is yours, and yours alone, and that you are not in the habit of being disturbed during the night by tiny people climbing in to share it. Certainly, you do not want to go to bed to enjoy a quiet, or passionate, night with your partner, only to find yourself usurped by the baby or toddler, or sometimes even reduced to sleeping in your child's bed.

Your attitude to sleep

Finally, don't forget that your own attitude to sleep will influence your behaviour when dealing with your child's sleep issues. So ask yourself a few questions about your sleep habits before you tackle those of your child.

What are your own sleeping routines? If you sleep erratically and don't keep regular hours, do you need to take a different approach for your children? Are you anxious about your own sleep? Is this impacting on the way you approach your baby's sleep routines? When your baby came along, was the prospect of sleepless nights one of the things that you worried about? Or did you accept that a natural part of being a new mum would be suffering sleep deprivation in one form or another? Do you get irritable and bad-tempered if you don't have enough sleep?

Look at your responses to these questions and you will probably give yourself the reason to get your baby into a good sleep routine so everyone in the household can have a sound night's sleep. The next step is tackling the problem, and this is where this book aims to help you.

Start with the recognition that you, the parent, are not approaching the issue of sleep in a neutral way. You are heavily ego-involved – and this may affect your judgement. You may be anxious about your own sleep, or concerned that you plan to return to work and so getting your baby into a routine before you do so is essential. But try to relax: the first rule of less stressful parenting is that a relaxed mother is more likely to have a relaxed baby and, temperament aside, a relaxed baby is often likely to sleep well, too.

So, is there a problem?

If you've bought this book, chances are that there is some aspect of your child's sleep habit that you are concerned about. Below is a number of questions for you to answer, and the answers will give you an indication as to whether your child has a sleep issue.

The good news is that every one of these issues will be addressed in this book and there is something you can do to improve them.

○ When you put him to bed, does your child refuse to stay there?

○ Does your child fall asleep most nights in front of the television, on the sofa, or in a pushchair?

○ When he goes to bed, does he keep calling for you?

○ Does your child come to your room in the middle of the night on a regular basis?

- Does your baby fall asleep only if you are holding him?
- Is your child waking in the middle of the night for a feed?
- Does your child come to your bed in the night and insist on sharing?
- Is your child sleeping with you while your husband sleeps in your child's bed?
- Is your child waking several times in the night and crying for you?
- Does your child come downstairs after you have put him to bed?
- Is your child's bedtime getting progressively later and is he tired in the morning?
- Does your child refuse to sleep unless you stay in the room?
- Is he awake for long periods at night?
- Do you and your partner argue about your child's sleeping habits?
- Do you have negative feelings or feel apprehensive when it's time for your child to go to bed?
- Are you exhausted from waking up in the middle of the night?

Don't forget

o Good sleep is as important to a growing child as good food.

o Babies have more REM sleep than adults, which scientists believe is important for brain development.

o Hormones are released during sleep which promote growth and development.

o Babies of less than six weeks old have very erratic sleep–wake patterns.

o Sleep requirements vary from child to child, and 10–15 per cent of children do not conform to the average for their age.

o By 12 weeks sleep is settled into regular patterns of long night-time sleep and two naps during the day.

o To reinforce light–dark associations, always put your baby to sleep in a darkened room.

o Put the baby down to sleep when he is drowsy but still awake so he gets used to falling asleep in his cot.

o For a baby between the ages of 8 and 15 months, sleep routines may be disrupted by separation anxiety.

o Routines make a child feel safe in a predictable world.

And so to bed – getting ready for sleep

What is a good sleeping routine?

Throughout this book a lot of emphasis will be laid on the importance of establishing a good sleep routine. This is the first step in improving your child's – and your – sleep habits. A routine doesn't have to be complicated; it can just be as simple as a bath, stories and bedtime, and so on, but it does need to be regular and consistent. A child with a good bedtime routine knows what to expect, is comforted by the routine and looks forward to bedtime.

A good sleep routine should incorporate the following:

Getting enough sleep

It seems obvious to say, but for children to be happy and healthy they need enough sleep. Children need a certain amount of sleep to replenish their energy for another day and in order to build their body and mind.

The actual amount of sleep they require varies between individuals, but the charts on pages 26–9, which show the average hours recommended for children of specific ages, will give you an idea of what is appropriate for your child. Of course, these recommendations are only averages and it may be that your child sleeps more or less, and this is where it is important to know your child and to trust your parental instinct as to whether you think she is getting enough sleep. For example, an average six-month-old will sleep for 14 out of 24 hours (including naps), but 10 per cent of children will sleep considerably less.

Shape your child's sleep

Sleep is most beneficial for a child if it is undisturbed and follows your child's natural inclinations – and this is particularly true in the early months. As your child gets older, though, and you find yourself shaping her routine to fit in with that of the family, you may have to interrupt a long sleep in the late afternoon, to make sure that she will still be tired enough later to be able to go to bed at night at a reasonable hour.

Sleeping at the right time

Hanging in the window of a local shop is a baby's t-shirt which has a message on it that says, *'I'm so tired, I could stay awake all night.'* An adult who gets very tired tends to droop and become more lethargic, whereas once children are over-tired, many become more rather than less active and their behaviour can be described as 'wired'.

For infants this change – from tired to over-tired – shows itself in fussiness, becoming irritable, crying and rejecting all soothing efforts made by their parents. Toddlers will start to exhibit more disruptive behaviour and they tend to run around, getting more and more excited until they collapse in an exhausted heap. Watch your child and note when she droops; it is at this point that you need to get her ready for bed. If that 'window' passes, she will get a second wind and become over-tired and difficult to settle.

Once your baby drops her afternoon nap you might find it necessary to put her to bed earlier in the evening and to increase the amount of her night-time sleep, rather than reduce her overall quantity of sleep. Paradoxically, this is particularly true if your baby gets into the habit of waking early: rather than keeping her up longer in the evening, it is better to put her to bed earlier.

Ensure your child has regular sleep

For the first few weeks of life a baby's 'routine' is unpredictable and uncertain; babies drift in and out of sleep with little or no pattern, so the best advice for a parent at this stage is to follow their child's lead.

Once your child begins to sleep longer at night (from around six weeks old), a discernable pattern starts to evolve and you can begin to plan your day around your baby's naps. By the age of about two, most infants will have given up their morning nap, and by the age of three or four they will not sleep during the day at all. At this point a child should be sleeping in a predictable and regular way and parents can be confident that their child's sleep needs are being met.

Establish a regular bedtime and rising time

By setting regular times for going to bed and getting up in the morning you will ensure that both you and your child have similar expectations, and it will also allow you to plan

Routine, routine

Regularity does not mean that the baby will always be sleepy at the same time each day. Circadian rhythms are 25 hours long, not matching the 24-hour day, so occasionally children will not be tired on cue. Nor will they always wake up on cue. Unstructured, our normal daily rhythms would tend to drift out of sync with the 24-hour day if it were not for external cues, such as a set bedtime, a bedtime routine, lightness and darkness. This is why a regular routine is important, as it helps keep your child's internal body clock, or circadian rhythm, on a 24-hour cycle.

a bedtime routine accordingly. Without this structure your child may end up going to bed later and later, leading to chronic sleep deprivation. For babies, the regularity of a going-to-bed routine creates a sense of order and stability in the household, which contributes to making her feel secure. Indeed, for children of all ages, a predictable world is a safe world.

Having a fixed bedtime suits children who are by nature, natural followers of rules. Even children who are less receptive to rule-following like order and regularity in their life. A predictable world is a safe world. Children thrive on a sense that they have a regular bedtime and that they will wake up at a particular time to go to school or nursery, but this doesn't mean that you can't be flexible when the situation demands it. Children will enjoy having a later bedtime on special occasions, holidays or weekends, or an earlier

It's up to you!

There are many factors to consider as you choose where your baby will sleep. You'll know you've made the right choice when everyone in the family sleeps comfortably and your child gets the sleep she needs to grow and develop successfully.

one if they feel unwell or are particularly tired. My son, at the age of seven, was bathed, in his pyjamas and ready for bed. He kept asking me, 'What time is it?' In the end I asked him, 'Are you tired? Do you want to go to bed?' and he said, with great relief, 'Yes!' Good little boy that he was, he was trying to stay awake for his 'official' bedtime!

Where is the best place for your child to sleep?

Families make many choices about how they will care for their children, and where they sleep is one of them. In different parts of the world there are different theories about where a child should sleep, with the majority of infants in non-western societies sleeping alongside their parents. In western societies most parents expect that in time their child will sleep alone in a cot or a bed in their own bedroom, but the issue here is, when? Should the baby be in its own room from birth? Or should she be moved out of the parents' room after six months, as recommended by some experts? Or perhaps she should go into a bedroom when the child decides she is ready, or when the parents feel the time is right?

Where a baby sleeps is a very personal decision. In some families parents and babies share the same bed – which is referred to as co-sleeping – but other parents may decide that babies should sleep in their own cots and in a different room. If you are trying to decide where your young baby will sleep, there are a few things you should consider.

Co-sleeping

Some parents choose to sleep with their baby or child in the same bed. This decision can be made for practical reasons, such as having limited bedroom space in their home, or a difficult-to-soothe baby, or they may want the closeness that sharing sleep time provides.

These are some of the arguments that are often put forward in favour of co-sleeping:

o It allows more time for the family to be together and helps parents to bond with their baby.

o Skin-to-skin contact soothes the baby and helps promote sleep.

o It is more convenient for breastfeeding during the night.

o Babies are quickly and easily comforted and less likely to cry for prolonged periods.

o It helps babies who are hard to settle to learn to do so.

However, there are also arguments put forward against co-sleeping, which include:

- There is a question about the safety of co-sleeping.
- Babies learn to settle more easily without the distraction of other people around them.
- A baby is more likely to learn to self-soothe if she is sleeping in her own cot.
- Parents may find it difficult to sleep if they have a baby

SIDS and sleep safety

Sudden infant death syndrome (SIDS) is the unexplained death of a baby during sleep. The majority of deaths that are due to SIDS occur before six months of age, but the risk can extend into the toddler years.

Research has shown that putting babies to sleep on their back decreases the risk of SIDS. It is also recommended that babies should sleep on a firm surface, without soft bedding such as pillows or duvets, and in the 'feet-to-foot' position (baby's feet against the foot of the cot), so that there's less chance of slipping down beneath the bedding.

The baby should also sleep in a smoke-free room where the temperature should be well controlled, and parents should also make sure their baby does not get too hot, by checking her and ensuring that she does not have too many blankets or covers.

with them, especially parents who themselves have sleep issues.

○ It restricts the intimate life of the parents.

○ Infants who co-sleep learn to associate sleep with being in the parents' bed, which may become a problem at nap-time or when she needs to go to sleep before the parents.

○ What works with a baby will be less comfortable with a vigorous toddler straggled across the bed.

The Avon SIDS research group, headed by Professor Peter Fleming of Bristol University, conducted studies into the sleeping position of pre-term and low-birth weight in-fants and they found that the risk of sleeping in a position other than on the back (in other words, either on the front or on the side) was associated with an increased risk of SIDS, especially for pre-term infants. They also found that the risk of SIDS from bed-sharing was significant for both term and pre-term infants if the mother was a smoker. For pre-term infants or infants who weighed less than 2.5kg at birth, bed-sharing carried a risk of SIDS even if the mother was not a smoker.

Babies could also suffocate if they sleep on the chest of an adult lying on a sofa, or similar, because they could slide between the back of a sofa and the adult's body or be smothered by the adult if he should roll over.

Is co-sleeping safe?

Supporters of co-sleeping argue that, in most non-western cultures, co-sleeping is the most common way for babies to sleep. However, differences in mattresses, bedding and other cultural practices are thought to account for the lower risk of death and injury to young children that occur in these countries.

In the UK, the Foundation for the Study of Infant Deaths (FSID) recommends that the safest place for a baby to sleep, for the first six months, is in her own crib or cot in a room with her parents. The Consumer Product Safety Commission (CPSC) in the USA goes so far as to warn parents not to place their infants to sleep in adult beds, stating that the practice puts babies at risk of suffocation and strangulation. Their argument is further strengthened by the support of the American Academy of Pediatrics (AAP), which is in agreement with the CPSC.

The CPSC identifies four primary hazards that face infants sleeping in an adult bed:

O Suffocation caused by an adult rolling on top of or next to a baby.

O Suffocation when an infant gets trapped or wedged between a mattress and headboard, nightstand, wall or other rigid object.

O Suffocation resulting from a baby being face down on a mattress or on soft bedding such as pillows, blankets or quilts.

O Strangulation in a headboard or footboard that allows

part of an infant's body to pass through and then traps the baby's head.

Co-sleeping advocates dispute these risks, however, main-taining that the practice is not inherently dangerous and that is highly unlikely that parents will roll over onto a baby because they're conscious of her presence – even during sleep.

Remember, though, that there is a difference between parents who co-sleep from choice, and start off with their baby in their bed, and those who did not intend that their child sleep with them but fall into the habit as a way of deal-ing with their child's night-time waking or failure to settle easily. For these parents co-sleeping is the solution to a problem, but, unfortunately, this 'solution' may become a problem in its own right. Research suggests that those who are 'reactive co sleepers' (in other words, they do it to solve a problem) may find it difficult to move their child back to her own bed when they have had enough of this situation.

So the lesson is: if you don't want your child to get into the habit of sleeping with you, don't start – however tempt-ing it is in the middle of the night to bring your wandering child into bed with you.

Moving from parents' bed to cot

Moving a child from the parental bed, or even a crib in the parent's bedroom, to a cot is best done at around the age of six months – before the co-sleeping habit has become

Co-sleeping safety rules

If you do opt to sleep with your baby in your bed, bear in mind some of the following rules:

O Never sleep with a baby in your bed if you have been drinking alcohol or taking drugs – including prescribed drugs that make you drowsy.

O Don't co-sleep with a baby if you are a smoker, even if you never smoke in the bedroom or in the house.

O Don't share the bed if your baby was either premature (born before 37 weeks), had a low birth weight (less than 2.5kg) or is less than three months old.

O Don't share your bed with a small baby and a toddler; such a young child is unlikely to be aware of the baby's presence.

O Always place your baby on her back to sleep and leave her head uncovered.

O Make sure your bed's headboard and footboard don't have openings or cutouts that could trap your baby's head.

O Make sure your mattress fits snugly into the bed frame to prevent your baby becoming trapped in between the frame and the mattress.

O Don't put a baby down to sleep in an adult bed on her own or unattended.

O Don't use pillows, duvets, quilts or other soft or plush items on the bed.

ingrained and other issues (such as separation anxiety) come into play.

The co-sleeping routine will be broken at some point, either naturally, because the child decides to sleep alone, or by the parents' choice. Parents often become less keen to share their bed with their child when she grows into an energetic toddler who moves around while they are trying to get a good night's sleep!

When a new baby arrives it may not be convenient or safe for the baby to have a lively toddler sharing the bed.

How do sleep problems arise?

Sleep problems begin in a variety of ways. One of the most common causes amongst small children starts with their unwillingness to fall asleep alone. A bad habit usually arises after the parents 'solve' the problem of their baby crying before bedtime by rocking, cuddling or feeding her until she falls asleep. For the baby, falling asleep alone is now impossible. In order to fall asleep she has to be rocked, cuddled or fed.

Older mobile children often have problems associated with night waking, too. All children 'wake' in the night – not necessarily fully, but partially. Most children learn to pass through that phase and are able to go back to sleep without any parental intervention. Where an issue arises is if the child wakes fully and requires her parents to

New advice on dummies for parents

The Foundation for the Study of Infant Deaths (FSID) announced in June 2007 that settling your baby to sleep with a dummy – even for naps – can reduce the risk of cot death. If you use a dummy while your child sleeps, don't worry if the dummy falls out while she is asleep. However, if you are breastfeeding, don't give a dummy until your baby is one month old, to ensure that breastfeeding is well established. Never force your baby to take a dummy if she doesn't want it, and don't coat it in anything sweet to encourage her to take it.

soothe her back to sleep. The key to solving this problem is setting up good habits in the first place, building them into a routine and then sticking to it. Easier said than done, sometimes!

Unstructured sleep routines

Often parents underestimate the importance of sleep and good sleep habits. They take the view that since their baby sleeps anywhere and everywhere they do not have much control over their child's routine and so they make less effort to establish a routine. Although it is true that very small babies sleep erratically, older children need their body clock to be synchronized with that of the household if they are to get enough sleep. It is the parents who have the responsibility of making sure that their child's sleep patterns and eating habits are regularized.

Keeping baby up

Working parents in particular will often keep their baby up past her 'natural' sleeping time, so that they can spend time with her when they come home. A baby who is denied her bed when really she is ready for it will easily become over-tired and fretful and often the parents will find themselves having to soothe, rock or hold her before she can fall asleep. This in itself can set up a whole new range of problems.

Sometimes a baby's naps are sacrificed to fit in with the after-school and extra-curricular activities of siblings; babies who are ferried around in this way will frequently fall asleep in the car or the pushchair for short periods of time. Unless it is a long journey, this catnapping is not a replenishing form of sleep and if being moved in and out of a car, the baby will often be wakened again for another trip, disturbing her sleep even more.

Reactions to crying and fretfulness

If a baby becomes fretful and over-tired, a parent may compound sleeping problems by rocking, holding or soothing her. It's a natural instinct to comfort a baby when she cries, and we all feel like bad parents if we don't do something to calm her and make her happy. However, when a baby cries and is fretful because she is over-tired, the best response is not to rock, sing to or pat the baby. What she actually needs is to be put down in the cot and allowed to fall asleep on her own.

If a child falls asleep in the 'wrong place'

Sometimes if they are struggling to get their child to sleep in her cot and she won't do it immediately, parents resort to soothing the child to sleep wherever they are – perhaps in front of the television, in the car or in a pushchair. Although this solves the problem in the short term, in the long term it will set up wrong sleep associations for the child and is often the start of more enduring sleep problems.

Temporary changes

Any minor or major changes to daily life, such as holidays, illness or teething, can disrupt a well-established pattern of sleep and routine will go out of the window. At this point, because they themselves have busy lives or are tired from dealing with sleepless nights, parents will often take a short cut to get their child to sleep by letting her fall asleep downstairs or in their bed. It takes only a few days for the child to associate these new activities with being a way of falling asleep and she will quickly become reluctant to go back to her old methods. The habit of falling asleep in a cot or crib is easily replaced by the habit of falling asleep downstairs or in mummy's bed.

Bedrooms, cots, beds and bedding

If you are having your first child, the options available for kitting out the nursery can be overwhelming. There are a few things that are essential to help promote good sleep for your child and provide a safe and cosy environment in which to sleep. Let's start with the general atmosphere for the bedroom.

Bedroom

To create a safe place for your baby, and a bedroom in which she will relax and sleep, take the following factors into account:

Quiet

Although small babies will sleep almost anywhere when they are tired, it is a good idea to get them used to falling asleep in their own cot in their own room early on in their life. This is the beginning of training your child into good sleeping habits, and it will pay dividends for you later.

The right temperature

It is important that a child should not get too hot while sleeping, because of the danger of SIDS (see pages 46–7). If you are using blankets in the cot and the central heating is on throughout the house, make sure the baby's bedroom isn't too warm.

The temperature in the room ideally should be between 16 and 20ºC; buy a room thermometer to keep an eye on the temperature. It is also a good idea to check physically if your baby is sweating or feels hot to the touch. A baby who is red in the face and has damp hair is a baby who is too hot. If she is, you should adjust her clothing or bedding. Turn off the radiator or turn the thermostat down, or remove a blanket.

When you put your baby to bed, cover her lightly, then, as you go to bed and the central heating goes off, add an extra blanket.

Dark

As light becomes dark, the brain produces a chemical, called melatonin, which induces sleep. To keep the dark–light cycle strong, make sure your child's room is dark when she goes to bed at night – turn off overhead lights and leave on only a dim nightlight or a landing light. To keep the room dark in the long summer evenings, buy 'black-out' curtains to exclude as much light as possible.

Conversely, in the morning, the room should be light to turn off the melatonin and help your child to wake up.

No distractions

If you have older children, do not let them have televisions, games consoles or DVD players in their bedrooms. It might surprise you to know that a significant percentage of four-year-olds have televisions in their rooms, but this is not a good idea: in a recent survey among a group of American 4–10-year-olds, a television in a child's bedroom was the most powerful predictor of overall sleep disturbance and bedtime resistance.

Cot

When choosing a cot or a crib for your infant, there are a few safety and comfort features that you should bear in mind, but, most important, buy it from a reputable dealer and make sure it conforms to British standard BSEN716. Most cots will have a sticker or label to this effect. If you are buying a new cot, things to consider include:

○ In the UK, the recommendation is that spaces between bars or slats on the sides must be 45–65mm, and less than 60mm wide in the mattress base.

○ Corner posts should be no higher than 1.5mm.

○ Avoid sharp edges, exposed hardware, or splintered wood.

○ Painted cribs must not have been decorated using lead-based paint.

○ Ensure all screws and bolts are present and tightly secured (and this is important whether you are buying a cot made up or if you are assembling it yourself).

○ Check that the mattress support is securely attached to the headboard and footboard.

○ Make sure the mattress fits snugly into the cot frame. You shouldn't be able to fit more than two finger widths between the mattress and the cot sides.

○ If you buy a cot with sides that drop down (useful if you are having the cot next to your bed for night feeding, or if you have had a Caesarean and lifting is tricky), check that the drop-side latches are unreachable by children or are difficult to release, making them child-safe.

Safety first

If you are given a cot, or inherit an old family one, be warned that it may not conform to current safety standards: for example, it may be painted with lead-based paint. So always check that it complies with the rules and safety standards for new cots.

O Make sure the base of the cot is adjustable so that you can set the mattress to its highest position until your baby is able to sit up unsupported or can pull herself up, then lower it as your child grows and becomes more adventurous! When the cot is set for a newborn, the cot sides or end need to be at least 500mm higher than the mattress.

Positioning a cot or a crib

O Keep the cot clear of curtains or blind cords, which may be a strangulation hazard. If you can't, shorten curtains and cords so they are out of reach of exploring hands.

O Keep the cot well away from heaters and power points.

O There should not be any mirrors or pictures on the wall above the cot which could fall down on the baby.

Mattress/cot bumpers

When buying a new mattress, look for a kite-mark label or sticker that says it complies with safety standards. Make sure the mattress fits the cot snugly – there should be no more than two fingers' width between the mattress and cot sides.

You may want to use cot bumpers in your nursery as a final cosy touch to the whole look, but before you do, bear in mind that there are concerns about their safety. Cot bumpers attach to the inside of the cot to keep the cot draught-free and protect the baby from pushing its head against the sides. However, they can restrict the flow of air across the cot, causing the baby to get too hot. A more serious worry is that they may come loose and cover the baby's head, resulting in suffocation. If you do use a cot bumper, make sure it is well secured, check it regularly and also ensure that the room temperature is well controlled. When your baby is able to stand, remove the bumper so that she cannot use it as a ladder to climb out of the cot.

Bedding

Chose bedding that fits firmly to a bed or cot – fitted sheets are best – and use cotton sheets for babies and young children as they are cooler. Purchase a couple of cotton cellular blankets for babies, as these allow air to circulate which

Cosy toes

If the cot sheets are cold, place a warm towel or muslin cloth on the mattress to take off the chill. But do remove it before you put your baby to bed.

means she will not overheat if one gets wrapped around her body.

If your child is a restless sleeper and kicks off her bedding in the night, she will feel cold in the early morning. A baby sleeping bag is a good solution, and has the bonus of keeping her in bed when she is old enough to climb out! Wait until she is a few months old to put her in one, or big enough that her head won't slip through the hole and slide down into the bag, which could cause suffocation.

Top tips for moving your child from cot to bed

O Put the bed in your child's bedroom alongside her cot before you make the move from cot to bed, and give your child time to adjust to the idea.

O Don't disassemble the cot until you can see that your child is content with the new arrangement.

O If you are not using rails, either put a mattress directly on the floor for the first few nights, or put a layer of cushions next to the bed to soften the landing when your child falls out of bed – because she will!

O If possible, choosing a bed that incorporates raised edges is ideal as it presents a small – but important – barrier to encourage your child to stay in her bed.

O Think about putting a stair gate on the bedroom door to stop her wandering around at night or in the early

Moving your child from a cot to a bed

Another common question from parents is when should you move your baby from a cot to a bed? There's no clear answer to this question – it's simply a case of doing what's right for your child. Some people move their children out of a cot as early as 15 months, while others have children of three or three and a half who are still content to be in their cots. The rule of thumb is that when you think your

morning. If you don't like the idea of a gate, but you have a child who may go downstairs alone, try fixing a bell over her door so you will hear her when she leaves the room.

O Present the move as an exciting step towards growing up. Involve your child in the choice of bed and bedding and encourage her to see this as a great treat.

O Don't make the move when there is a new baby due as this will only increase the sense of being displaced. Many children regress when there is a new baby in the house, and that may mean she wants her cot back.

O Try to tackle one change at a time. If your child is getting used to a new baby in the family, weaning from the bottle, adjusting to a new childcare situation or starting toilet training, hold off on the switch to a bed for a while until things settle down.

baby can escape from a cot, it's no longer safe for her to be in it.

When you do move your child from a cot to a bed, another thing you might consider is whether to use a bed guard or rails on the bed.

Again, this is a matter of choice. Some parents find it a necessity for their child, others are happy without. However, rails can be a good buffer zone between a cot and a bed – preventing the child from falling out in the night and also providing her with a sense of security (as well as an incentive to stay in the bed!). You may not need to use them for long so, if possible, borrow them from a friend.

Bunk beds: good idea?

The Child Accident Prevention Trust recommends that the top bunks of bunk beds should not be used by children who are under six years old; Australian safety experts recommend that children do not sleep in bunk beds until they are nine years old. Never let children use bunk beds as a play area, as many injuries occur when children fall from the top bunk in such situations.

If you do decide to buy a bunk bed, select one that has a sticker stating that it complies with the mandatory standards. Make sure, too, that there are no gaps sized 95mm to 230mm in any part of the bed, including guardrails, so as to prevent children trapping their heads.

On the upper bed, guardrails or bed-ends should be at least 160mm above the top of the mattress, to prevent children rolling out. Check that any ladders are firmly fixed and stable and all tube ends on metal tubular bunk beds are plugged. Make sure that all nuts and bolts are flush and smooth, and there are no protrusions of more than 8mm that could catch onto clothing.

Don't forget

o Your child's room should be safe, quiet and dark. If she dislikes the dark, switch on a nightlight in her room or a landing light.

o Keep an infant's room temperature constant and verging on the cool side – especially if you have a young baby.

o Make sure your child is not hungry when she goes to bed. A child over six months old does not need food and drink in the night if she has fed well during the day.

o Make sure that everyone who looks after your child sticks to the same bedtime routine.

o Avoid stimulating activity before bed.

o Avoid creating bad sleep associations. Encourage your child to fall asleep in her own bed, without you.

o Experts recommend that a baby sleeps in her own cot in her parents' room for the first six months. If you are co-sleeping, be aware of the safety issues.

o It is normal to wake partially during transitions from deep to light sleep.

o Set times for sleeping and eating help synchronize your baby's body clock with the household routine.

o If your child is three to three and a half years old and falls asleep in the afternoon, don't let her nap too long.

o When on holiday or staying with friends or family, try to stick to your bedtime routine wherever possible.

Getting into a
sleep routine

A good routine for bedtime should be one that involves a predictable wind-down at the end of the day which lets your child know that bedtime is approaching. This should include a series of events that happen in the same order every night and which take approximately the same amount of time (see page 83). When a child follows a regular routine, you will find he goes to bed calmly and looks forward to the process of going to sleep, so he should fall asleep without a fuss.

This doesn't happen by magic, though; it is up to you to introduce regular activities so that the baby's biological clock is brought into sync with the family routines. Just as a parent shapes their baby's eating habits to coincide with those of the rest of the family (by encouraging him to eat at regular times with a minimum of fuss), they can shape the sleeping habits of the baby too.

Sleep in the first year

The age at which babies settle themselves to sleep – meaning that they fall asleep quickly on their own and stay asleep – varies widely. Some babies will go to sleep without a problem but won't stay asleep; others may go to sleep with difficulty but then stay asleep; whereas other exhausting babies neither want to go to sleep nor stay asleep. Sadly, you can't predict what sort of baby you will have.

As a new parent, you will find yourself bombarded with advice on sleeping and you may well be told about approaches to sleep training that recommend parents follow a strict regime set by the clock. If your baby can be coaxed into such a routine, all well and good, but if you have a baby who is difficult to settle, you might do better to trust your own instincts and do what works for you and your baby instead.

Either way, any routine you try to impose before the age of six weeks will work only if it matches your baby's innate sleeping rhythms. There are a few things you can look for in your own baby's mannerisms and habits which might help you to understand his sleep patterns and so help to create a routine which will work well for him.

Is baby ready for bed?

When a baby is tired his eyelids will droop as he begins to fall asleep; his eyes will then close completely, but his eyelids will continue to flutter and his breathing will still be irregular. His hands and limbs will be flexed and he may startle, twitch and show fleeting smiles called 'sleep grins' – he may even continue a flutter-like sucking.

Often at this point the parent will go to put the baby down in his cot and as she does so he will suddenly startle and begin to cry. Most often this happens because he wasn't fully asleep at that point; he was still in a state of light sleep. Babies tend to spend longer in this earlier stage of sleep than older children and adults, and it may take them up to 20 minutes to move from light sleep into a deeper sleep.

Why timing is everything

If you try to rush your baby to bed while he is still in the initial light-sleep period, he will usually awaken as his head touches the mattress, so it is important to learn to recognize your baby's sleep stages. If you wait until your baby is in a deep-sleep stage before moving him from one sleeping place to another – such as from your bed to a crib or from car seat to bed or crib – the transition will be more successful and he should stay asleep. By three months things will become easier as baby goes into sleep more quickly, bypassing the lengthy light-sleep stage.

So how can you tell the difference between light sleep and deep sleep? Generally when baby enters a stage of deeper sleep, the facial twitching stops and his breathing will become shallower and more regular and his muscles will completely relax. Hands that were clenched into little fists will unfold and his arms will drop and dangle weightlessly. It is at this point that he is in a deeper sleep and unlikely to stir as you put him down.

Sometimes a baby will move through the drowsy sleepy stage and become irritable and fretful and start to cry. This type of crying is often difficult to calm, as the infant is overtired and simply needs to be settled down and left to fall asleep. Unfortunately what many parents do at this stage is to try to stop the crying in ways that work well when their baby is awake and alert. So parents will rock him, sing to him, try to engage him – all to no avail. The last thing the baby wants while in this state is more stimulation; he just wants to be left in peace to fall asleep. The best way to approach this problem is to put the baby in his cot, make shushing noises or rub his tummy and you should find that he will fall asleep again.

Sleep and babies

- **Babies don't sleep as deeply as you do.**
- **They take longer to go to sleep.**
- **They have twice as much active, or lighter, sleep as adults.**
- **They have more periods of wakefulness in the night.**

The first three months

In the first few weeks of life a baby will sleep erratically throughout the day and night. Trying to establish a routine before six weeks is generally unlikely to succeed, although it is worth trying to get your baby used to falling asleep in his cot and not in your arms, in a pushchair or in front of the television, even at this early age. When you put the baby into his crib or cot, turn off the light to get him used to the idea that a darkened room is a signal for going to sleep.

Newborn sleep

Every baby is different: some need more sleep than others, but on average a young baby should spend between 14 and 16 hours a day sleeping.

At around six weeks your baby's circadian rhythms will become established (if he was full-term) and so he should begin to sleep for longer stretches at night and be more awake during the day. Premature babies may take longer, however, as sleep patterns will match their expected date of birth rather than their actual date of birth. Before this time it may be difficult to get your baby to sleep during the night, but don't worry: it will pass.

From six weeks onwards most babies will be having their longest sleep at night, plus two or three daytime naps. Between 7 and 12 weeks most babies tend to develop a reasonable pattern of sleep. If you're lucky, your baby may settle around 11 p.m. and sleep through until the next feed, at around 4 a.m.

At three months old, a baby should average five hours of sleep during the day and 10 hours at night, usually with

Colic

In the early weeks your baby may become colicky and cry for prolonged periods – this often happens in the evening. Such behaviour can be very upsetting for parents, who feel that they are doing something wrong. However, it's not called 'three-month colic' for nothing; at around this point it often magically disappears as the baby's brain begins to produce the hormone melatonin, which induces drowsiness and relaxes the muscles surrounding the gut.

an interruption or two. About 90 per cent of babies of this age will sleep through the night – meaning sleeping for six to eight hours without waking.

Attachment and separation anxiety

In the second half of his first year a baby will show signs of becoming attached to his principal caregiver – usually his mother. This close bonding starts at around eight months and continues to grow, peaking at about 12 months. As heart-warming as this is, the downside of this attachment is the fear of separation from his carer, which affects some children more than others. If you have a baby who becomes anxious when he is separated from you, one of the points at which it shows itself will be at bedtime.

This behaviour may worsen if something happens to unsettle your baby. Any significant change in the household or family may make your baby feel insecure, especially if it takes either parent away from home. If you have started work again or if your child changes carers, if you have to go away from home or are even moving home, all these things can affect a sensitive baby.

If your baby's sleep is disrupted, the best response is to show your understanding of what is happening and to be more relaxed in your bedtime routine. Don't let your baby cry for long periods of time; instead sit with him. This isn't going against all the rules and setting up bad habits – it's recognizing that your baby's needs have changed and he requires reassurance. Don't be inflexible. It is important not to interact or play with him, pick him up and soothe him or feed him; you just need to sit by the cot and place your hand gently on his tummy so that your presence alone is the comfort he needs to settle himself down to sleep.

Sleep associations

It is never to soon to develop consistent routines, as they will quickly play a major role in your child's ability to sleep soundly. The associations formed in the first few months and throughout the first year will become part of his expectations about how and where he will fall asleep. As I have said earlier, babies who are rocked to sleep will not learn to fall asleep unaided. Also, now that he is more interested in the world around him, it becomes more important to place him in a quiet, darkened room, where he will be able to sleep well and without distractions.

A point that cannot be emphasized strongly enough is that the process of going to bed every evening should be a calm and pleasurable one for a child; one that rounds off the day and prepares him for sleep. A predictable and regular bedtime routine also has the advantage of giving a child a sense of security and order in his daily life, and a sense that his parents are in charge.

So decide on a going-to-bed routine for your baby that will provide him with positive associations. Prepare him for bed with a warm bath and then get him into his pyjamas. Take him into his bedroom, give him a cuddle and perhaps sing him a little song, then tuck him in and leave. Your baby will probably fret a little at this stage, and may even cry, but don't rush in – leave him for a few minutes to see if he will settle by himself.

If a baby who is under six months old continues to cry for several minutes, it's time to respond. He may be genuinely uncomfortable: hungry, wet, cold, or even sick. So go back into his room and check that he is not uncomfortable, tuck him in again and repeat the routine. But don't engage with him: simply show him that you are there and that you will come to him when he is distressed, but do not fall into the trap of playing with him, feeding him or trying out new approaches which will confuse the existing routine. Make sure your partner is 'on-message' and does the same thing.

As your baby becomes more social (smiling, giggling and laughing) he may well prefer to be with you and to spend this time in the evening playing rather than going to sleep, so you may encounter some resistance to nap- and bedtimes. Do not give in, though – to do so will deny him the critical sleep he needs. Over-tired babies quickly become miserable, and many may cry with such duration and intensity that they even appear to be sick.

The format for establishing these good sleep associations varies a little depending on your baby's age:

Three to six months
During most of this period your baby will still be waking for night feeds. At around six months old babies will drop their three naps down to two, at which time (or earlier) they are

physically capable of sleeping through the night. If you are bottle-feeding, don't be tempted to give your baby extra formula to help him sleep – it won't work. By six months his length of sleep at night from his last feed should have increased to seven hours; so if the last feed is at 10 p.m., you can expect a wake-up at around 5 a.m.

Regular naps establish themselves during this period, too, as your baby's biological rhythms mature. The mid-morning nap usually starts at around 9 a.m. and might last about an hour; the early afternoon nap begins at 12 p.m. until about 2 p.m. and will probably last an hour or two, then your baby might have another nap in the late afternoon anywhere between 3 p.m. and 5 p.m. – which will vary in length. However, don't let the early afternoon nap start much later than 3 p.m. or you may find it messes up the rest of his sleep schedule later in the evening.

If your baby misses a nap, keep him up until the next sleep (although it may need to begin a bit earlier), but remember that an over-tired baby will have difficulty falling

Time for an early night

If your baby is clearly tired, don't keep him awake. Contrary to what you may think, earlier bedtimes allow your child to sleep later and more soundly. Keeping him up too late will increase, not decrease, night awakenings and other sleep-related problems.

asleep and staying asleep. When your baby drops his third nap, you may find he needs an earlier bedtime.

Six to twelve months

Your baby can be eased into a 12-hour sleep at night by having a short nap in the morning and a longer one in the afternoon. Keeping your child up during the day doesn't necessarily make him sleep better; in fact, it usually makes him over-tired and irritable so that he fights sleep at night.

While up to 15 hours' sleep is ideal, most infants up to 11 months old get only about 12½ hours' sleep. Establishing healthy sleep habits is a primary goal during this period, as your baby is now much more social and his sleep patterns are more adult-like. The key is being sensitive to his sleep needs and adapting your lifestyle and scheduling your activities to be in sync with them. Babies at this stage may wake up early (5–6 a.m.) and go right back to sleep, or they may wake up a bit later (7 a.m.) to start the day. Whichever the case, there is little you can do to change this habit (such as by trying to keep him up later).

Sleep from one to three years

By the age of one, most children are settled into a good sleep routine. Toddlers need about 12–14 hours of sleep in a 24-hour period, and by about 18 months of age most toddlers will have only one nap in the afternoon, lasting between one and three hours. As with the younger child, the rule is still that naps should not occur too close to bedtime as they may delay him getting to sleep at night.

As your child becomes more active, curious and independent he may begin to resist going to sleep. Bedtimes with a toddler can be difficult; children of this age easily become over-tired and will move from being quiet and less active (seemingly sleepy), to being over-active and energetic. They will also vigorously resist any attempts to get them to sleep at this point, becoming more and more 'wired'.

At this age, there are several factors which conspire to create problems at bedtime that didn't exist before:

Increasing curiosity and independence

Toddlers are now discovering that there are so many interesting things and people to play with that staying up is much more fun than falling asleep. If you are a working mother it may be very tempting to keep your child up in the evening so that you can spend time with him, especially when he so obviously loves your company and is such a pleasure to be with. However, do try to have your time with him *during* his bedtime routine rather than getting into active and exciting play with him that will leave him over-stimulated.

Separation anxiety

When it comes to sleep and toddlers, it's often one step forward and two steps back. Things may happen in your toddler's world that will cause him to revert and become afraid of being away from you: common causes include a new carer, a new house, or maybe a new sibling.

At these times of change it is even more important to be consistent and stick to your routine, but you will also need to take into account these disruptions and see how they are affecting your child. Just as with a younger baby, if your child is distressed when he is left to sleep alone, let him cry for a few minutes to see if he settles, but if he sounds as if he is really upset, don't leave him. Go in and reassure him by being near but, again, don't engage. Your presence should be enough to reassure him that you will come when he is unhappy and that he has not been abandoned.

Assertiveness and the 'terrible twos'

Welcome to the age at which your child begins to think and behave like an independent human being. Usually he does this by saying 'no' to everything, including going to bed. What to do? Well, try to avoid a head-on confrontation, as this will only make him over-stimulated and over-tired. Instead, offer 'alternatives' – although this won't always work. For example, 'Do you want to wear the red pyjamas or the blue ones?;' 'Shall we read this book or that one?;' 'Do you want Mummy to bath you, or Daddy?' Offering your child a choice gives him some feeling of independence – often just enough to solve the problem. Whatever you do, try not to give in to his demands just for the sake of a quiet life: it might be quiet now, but the problem has not been solved, only postponed.

Naps

As your child becomes more social and interested in playing
and exploring the world, taking a nap suddenly seems much
less appealing. However, don't let naptimes slip as naps
are important for a young child to prevent him becoming
fatigued; fighting this fatigue only results in a heightened
state of wakefulness which makes it harder for him to
fall asleep and stay asleep. If your child persistently misses
naps, his fatigue accumulates, creating a vicious cycle
which will have the knock-on effect of encouraging night-
time sleep problems to develop.

Most children from the age of about 21 to 36 months
still need one nap a day – which can be anything from one
to three-and-a-half hours long. A child of this age should
typically go to bed somewhere between 7 p.m. and 8 p.m.
and wake up between 6 a.m. and 8 a.m. It is important to be
regular (but not necessarily rigid) with bedtimes and naptimes and consistent with your routines or rituals.

The transition from two naps to one may be bumpy,
where one nap is not enough and two are too many. If this
is the case, try moving your child's bedtime a little earlier,
so that he is more rested and better able to skip the morning nap. Not every night will be unbroken, of course, so your
child may still need the occasional morning nap, especially
if he is unwell. If your child is sleeping well and is rested,
occasional changes in his daily routine are generally well
tolerated at this stage. If, on the other hand, he is not sleeping well, changes may cause quite a few problems.

Be consistent

The key to dealing with sleep issues successfully is consistency and persistence. Starting routines early in your child's life and consistently maintaining them prevents many problems later on and makes dealing with those that do occur much, much easier.

Children who are not in a good sleep routine by now will often develop sleep issues, including refusing to take naps, resisting going to sleep, night-waking, getting out of bed and getting up too early.

Sleep from three to six years

Children between the ages of three and six typically have between 10¾ and 12 hours' sleep per day. They will often go to bed around 7 8 p.m. and will wake up between 6 a.m. and 8 a.m., just as they did when they were younger. At the age of three some children still nap, while at five most are not. If they are still sleeping during the day, these naps will gradually become shorter. The good news is that new sleep problems do not usually develop after three years of age.

There may be many changes in your child's life at this stage, such as starting nursery school or a playgroup, so be sensitive to your child's sleep needs and be aware of

It's about quality and quantity

Getting both the proper quality and quantity of sleep is very important for your child's development. Poor sleep is associated with behaviour problems such as aggression, defiance, non-compliance, oppositional behaviour, acting up and hyperactivity.

how well rested he is. Starting nursery school often tires children out and they may be ready to go to bed earlier or feel the need to sleep later in the morning.

If your child is content to go to bed, sleeps well and is lively and alert in the morning, there is nothing to be concerned about, but don't eliminate naps if he is not ready. Both you and he will pay the price if you do.

Sleep from seven to twelve years

Sleep requirements for children of primary-school age and just over are between 10 and 11 hours per day. At these ages – when they are involved in many social, school and family activities – bedtimes become later and later, with most 12-year-olds going to bed at about 9 p.m. However, primary-school children still exhibit a range of bedtimes (anywhere between 7.30 and 10 p.m.) as well as total sleep times (from 9 to 12 hours, although the average is 9½ hours).

Some sleep experts are concerned that children of school age are not sleeping enough, and recent research shows that most children go to sleep at a later hour than their parents did at the same age.

How do you know if your school-age child is tired?

If you're not sure if your child is tired or there is another problem, make a note of the amount of sleep your child is getting and compare it with the averages for his age group (see pages 26–9). Of course, your child is not average and so he may need more or less sleep than is recommended, but this figure should act as a helpful benchmark for you.

The most telling indicator of all is your child's behaviour at the start of the day. Does he need to be woken in the morning? Is he grumpy and lethargic? Does his teacher say that he is often sleepy at school?

Sleep needs do not decrease as a child matures and they remain vitally important to your child's health, development and wellbeing throughout his formative years. Without the proper amount of sleep, your child will become increasingly sleepy during the day and his school work will inevitably be affected.

Children who have a history of sleep problems will see them persist as they get older – they do not 'outgrow' them. Without intervention by you, these problems will continue to plague them and in fact will be more ingrained as the years go by.

Creating a sleep routine

Starting a sleep routine early and being consistent with it are keys for success. It typically takes only a few days for a baby to learn to fall asleep unassisted, but it is up to you to maintain the schedule and routines so that these habits are not lost. The sound sleep that follows this perseverance is a gift to him and to you as well.

What are you aiming for?

Do you have reasonable expectations of your child as far as his sleep is concerned? You cannot expect your baby to go to bed early and sleep late when he is simply not ready for it. It may be that your child is one of the 10 per cent who needs less sleep than the average, and although you can get him to bed you cannot make him sleep.

So adjust your own expectations. Your child is not average: he is who he is and that is what you have to deal with. You may have a child who is by nature more fussy and temperamental. This kind of child is also difficult to get into a routine – and you may even feel that he never will. However, do persist, because it is these children who benefit most from a good sleep routine.

If you are a working parent it may be very important to you that your child's sleeping schedule fits into your schedule (it may also encourage you to begin a sleep routine earlier than a stay-at-home mother). If your child is a good sleeper, is easy-going and doesn't have any external reason for not falling asleep, being consistent might be enough.

Sometimes life gets too much and you might find yourself exhausted from working and/or caring for a child, but it is at these times that it is even more important that you stick to your routine and not deviate from it. It will be hard not to become anxious about your own lack of sleep, but try not to communicate your own anxiety to your baby.

A good routine

o Prepare your child for going to bed and give him a reminder 20 minutes before it is time and again 10 minutes before. Say things like, 'When you've finished colouring that picture it will be time to get ready for bed.'

o Avoid exciting stories or activities just before bedtime. A scary story or tickling your child won't help him wind down and get himself ready for sleep. Avoid certain television programmes in the hour before bed – some programmes are often too exciting or scary for children and they may carry their fears to bed with them (see pages 150–1).

o Start the bedtime routine with a warm, relaxing bath which is fun but not too boisterous, before getting him into his pyjamas and asking him to clean his teeth. Now he is ready to get into bed and start his going-to-sleep routine.

o When he is in his cot or his bed, sit and read a book to him. If you have a baby, he may prefer to hear a gentle lullaby or just the sound of your voice, low and reassuring. Once the reading is over, tuck your child in comfortably, give him a soft toy, a favourite blanket or dummy, say goodnight and leave.

O Be firm about the amount of reading you will do and don't give in to 'Just one more story, please!'

O Leave on a nightlight or landing light if he wants one; some children like to fall asleep to the sound of soft music or songs.

O Babies may grizzle a little but older children who are used to the routine should settle and fall asleep quickly.

O With an older child you may want to incorporate a little chat about the day's activities before you start the story, but don't make it too long.

O From bathtime to finish the whole routine should last approximately 30 minutes.

What to do if your baby doesn't settle

A reminder of you

Give him something that reminds him of you. A baby who finds it difficult to settle may be soothed by an item of clothing – say, your nightgown – which smells of you, or a recording of your voice.

A dummy

If your baby is used to feeding before he falls asleep, giving him a dummy which he can suck on contentedly may help – it's no surprise that the Americans call it a 'pacifier'! However, never put your baby to bed with a bottle of milk (breast or formula) or juice; both of these can cause 'baby-bottle tooth decay'.

Comfort objects

Many children have a blanket or piece of cloth which they hold close when they are tired or anxious. Two of my three children loved their baby blankets, especially the ones with a satin ribbon on the edge, which they took to bed until they started school.

Swaddling

This technique of wrapping a baby in a blanket mimics the closeness of the womb and has the effect of calming many newborn babies. Some mothers wrap their baby tightly in a blanket until he looks like a parcel, then place him gently in his cot. Other variations on this theme (particularly for older babies) involve tucking the baby in tightly with the blankets secured under the mattress.

White noise

Most babies are soothed by sounds, preferably ones that remind them of the womb. Research has shown that the ones they find most calming are rhythmic, monotonous, low-pitched and humming in quality, involving a sound pattern that repeats at a rate of 60 to 70 pulses per minute. There are number of products on the market that possess these qualities, but there are also lots of things around the house which have a similar effect:

○ Set the radio on a talk station (BBC Radio 4 is good) at a low volume.

○ Make a CD recording of running or dripping water, the

vacuum cleaner or the spin cycle of the washing machine.

○ Record simple lullabies, including your own made-up ones using your child's name.

○ If you have one, a metronome set at 60 beats per minute works well.

○ There are special CDs available to help babies fall asleep to the classics – and it might be easier on your ears, too!

How routine can be disrupted

Once a routine is established there is a number of things that may disrupt it. Some can be expected, such as the occasional illness or teething; others, such as holidays (sometimes with jet lag), moving house or the arrival of a new sibling, happen less often. As your child gets older, his imagination becomes very active and that can result in night-time fears of monsters and ghosts.

Older children may also react to tensions within the household which can result in their sleep being disrupted,

Bend the rules in times of trouble

If your child is ill, unhappy or distressed, don't leave him to cry; go to him and soothe him with your presence. If that doesn't work, pick him up and soothe him until he stops crying. Trust your instincts. Although a good routine is important, it shouldn't be at the expense of your child's happiness.

sometimes accompanied with bed-wetting as another sign of their anxiety. The golden rule is to try to keep to their routine as far as possible.

Finally, different individuals appear to have different rhythms: there are night owls and larks. Even within the same family there will be babies who appear to prefer to be awake at the end of the day and those who rise early in the morning.

When a lark is born into a family of owls, there is even more pressure to get the baby to adopt the sleeping patterns of the household. A good routine synchronizes the innate sleep rhythms of the child with the patterns of the household. Sometimes the child's body clock is very resistant to conforming with the household timetable, and it must be remembered that for some children sleep and waking time can be adjusted only so far. Such children will have their own routine – a predictable waking and sleeping schedule; it's just that it doesn't necessarily suit the other family members.

Don't forget

○ Look out for and learn the signs that your baby is tired and ready for bed.

○ Children easily become over-tired and are more rather than less energetic when tired.

○ Start to establish a routine as soon as possible, but don't be rigid with it in exceptional circumstances.

○ If your aim is to get your baby to sleep in his own bed without you being with him, don't get into the habit of staying until he falls asleep.

○ From six months on, your baby should be sleeping for most of the night and napping twice a day. At this age there is a structure to his sleep–wake pattern that will easily fit into a routine.

○ Increasing assertiveness of the under-threes brings a new set of problems, including bedtime resistance and tantrums. If you have well-established routine you are less likely to experience these problems.

○ A good routine should include a warning that bedtime is coming, followed by a bath, pyjamas, a story or song (or both), a cuddle and then a firm 'good night'.

○ Be consistent. Don't give in to any requests for 'just one more...'

○ When you leave, go without dithering. If your baby cries, wait to see what happens before returning.

I don't want to
go to bed!

The aim of getting your child to have a good night's sleep without interruption and in her own cot sometimes falters at the first hurdle. This is especially true if your baby doesn't want to settle and cries at length, or is an older child who resists going to bed or, once in bed, keeps getting up for various fabricated reasons. In other words, you may be able to get her *into* bed with the help of a good bedtime routine, but you have now become part of this routine, to the extent that the child won't go to sleep without you there. Whatever the scenario, your problem is how to get your child to settle herself to sleep without your help.

Settling baby

Apart from the obvious physical reasons – she is hungry, cold, wet or colicky – there are many reasons why a baby won't settle in the early evening, besides being over-tired.

'I'm so tired I could stay awake all night!'

When a baby becomes over-tired, what she needs is less stimulation, not more. Don't try to distract her from her crying by talking to her, rocking her vigorously or playing with her; instead, put her down and allow her to go to sleep. She may cry a little when she is first put into her cot, but she will quickly settle.

A few reasons why babies won't settle at night

Temperament

Not all babies are the same; some, by temperament, will be more difficult to put down to sleep than others. If you have a baby who is easily startled, cries frequently and is difficult to console, it's also likely that she will be difficult to settle at night. In this situation, keep her calm by reducing background noise and dimming the lights in the room. A difficult-to-settle baby *will* settle in time, but it will take longer to get her into a routine, so it is very important that you are consistent and patient.

Illness, teething and colic

If your baby is suffering, whatever the cause, treat the pain and comfort her by holding her. If she is colicky and cries every evening for a couple of hours, don't try to get her into a sleep routine; instead concentrate on calming her. Once she looks drowsy, put her down in her cot. (As discussed in Chapter 3, make sure she is in deep sleep before you do this, otherwise she will wake when you put her down.) To soothe her if she wakes up, put a comfort object in her cot, such as a blanket or a piece of clothing that smells of you.

Separation anxiety

Look out for the effects of separation anxiety, which often appear at around eight months (see page 71) and which may lead a baby who has previously settled without murmur

Snug as a bug...

A good tip is to warm the cot with a warm towel or one of those specially designed, animal-shaped bean bags you can heat in a microwave; do this before you put your baby down, so that the change in temperature doesn't disturb her. (But remember to remove it before you lay her down and touch the mattress to make sure it is not too hot.)

to fret and cry when left alone at night. Babies differ in the extent to which they experience separation anxiety, so there is no 'one size fits all' solution. If you have a sensitive and anxious baby, you may have to go in and reassure her that you have not abandoned her. When you go in, don't say anything, don't pick her up (unless she is distraught), but just sit by her cot and gently rub her tummy until she stops crying and falls asleep. Be sure to wait until she is in deep sleep before you go, otherwise she will be anxious about going to sleep if she thinks you will be leaving her.

What cues are the right cues?

If your baby has got used to falling asleep when being rocked, fed or with a parent alongside her, she will be unable to sleep when she is alone. In this situation, the best response is to try to change those associations by putting her in her cot while she is drowsy, but awake. She may wake and cry at first but, again, don't rush in immediately;

wait and see if she will settle on her own. If she persists in crying when she is left, though, use one of the methods described on pages 84–6 to help her to learn how to get herself off to sleep.

Bedtime resistance from one year onwards
New stage, new sleep challenges

A toddler who has been in a routine since she was a baby is less likely to resist going to bed. After all, at the end of the day she is tired and has a pleasurable routine to look forward to. Bedtime resistance does emerge in some children at around the age of two and can continue for years. There is a variety of reasons for this new behaviour, and several ways of dealing with it.

Staying up is more fun

Even a toddler in a well-established routine might occasionally try to extend her waking day, since she loves to have you to herself for a bit longer. She might ask for 'just one more story', call out that she wants to go to the toilet or ask for more water – anything to get you to come back to her. Resist her excuses, though, and firmly stick to your routine. If you start to give in to her requests, the process of 'asking for more' will continue. The whole point of a routine is that it doesn't change much – including the final stage, which is when she settles down and falls asleep.

Fear of the dark, strange noises, intruders or imagined ideas

When she is lying alone in the dark and perhaps isn't really tired enough to go to sleep at once, a child's imagination may run to fears and fantasies that are kept suppressed during a busy day. These fears are common in pre-school children and can be triggered by frightening television programmes, books or stories they have overheard. More than a third of children under the age of four (36 per cent) have a television in their bedroom, with 14 per cent having a DVD player too. Most sleep researchers advise against children having televisions in their bedrooms, as it has been proved that it interferes with their sleep patterns and is associated with behavioural problems.

If you child does wake at night in terror, never make light of her fear of monsters or burglars. Such things may seem fantastical to you, but they are very real to her and you should treat them accordingly. For more information on ways of dealing with these fears, see Chapter 5.

Lack of sleep or insomnia

Paradoxically, as children become more sleep-deprived they have more trouble falling asleep. As we have seen, they become energized and over-tired – apparently just the opposite of tired – but they *are* tired and they need to be put into a calm environment to go to sleep.

A very excitable child won't want to go to bed, so you may have 'tears before bedtime' or a tantrum when you suggest it. The trick here is not to let things reach this stage, but to anticipate when she is tired and to start a wind-down routine before she becomes sleepy.

Illness

When a child is ill she needs extra comfort. If your toddler has an ear infection, a tummy ache or some other complaint, give her the extra attention that she needs and adjust her bedtime routine accordingly.

Be sure to re-establish your old routine as soon as possible once the illness has passed, though. Don't worry if this takes some doing: it is only because your child will have got used to a new routine and enjoyed the extra attention at night.

Stress and anxiety

Children are no different from adults in that when they are feeling stressed or tense their sleep may be affected. Even babies are good at picking up on tension in the household or in their carers. So if you become anxious about your child's sleeping routine, she will pick up on that apprehension and her sleep will be affected.

The arrival of a new baby is another change that often causes a toddler to regress and resist going to bed, especially if she sees the new baby staying up with her parents while she has to go to bed alone. So try to be calm with your child in such situations and help her to feel secure and relaxed, even if you don't feel that way yourself!

Sleepy school-age children

Once your child starts school the existing routine of bath, getting dressed for bed, cleaning teeth, reading a story, having a cuddle and 'signing off' should continue. Perhaps somewhere you could add to this routine having a brief chat about the day. This may be the only opportunity you have in a busy life to stop and really listen to your child; and if she is worried about something, this is your chance to find out what that is.

Just because your child has a set bedtime doesn't necessarily mean that she will be sleepy at that time every night. If, on occasion, you sense your child is not ready to go to sleep at her usual bedtime, you could give her an additional 10 minutes with the light on so that she can read or listen to recorded stories or music until she is tired enough to sleep. Don't be tempted to give her a television or games console in her room, though, as this will only stimulate her further and delay her sleep. In an age when children have so many electronic gadgets, this is the perfect opportunity to establish a good reading habit.

Research has demonstrated the importance of good sleep and shown its link with educational achievement. A school-age child who has to be roused every morning, especially from a deep sleep, and who is often sleepy during the day, is sleep-deprived.

If your school-age child shows resistance to going to bed, consider whether the reason could be down to one of the following:

Is it the right bedtime?

If your child is going to bed and lying awake for more than 10–15 minutes, she may become anxious, prey to night-time fears and be unable to sleep *even if she is tired*.

If you are unsure as to what time is appropriate for a child of a certain age to be going to bed, consult the sleep chart on pages 26–9. This will help you establish what is the average length of night-time sleep for every age. (But don't forget that around 10 per cent of children will sleep either more or less than the average.) Working back from the time your child has to get up for school, subtract the amount of night-time sleep and ask yourself if she is going to bed too early for her age. If so, try keeping her up a little later.

As ever, be guided by your child: watch for signs of her becoming tired – yawning, slowing down – and move her bedtime in line with her natural sleep rhythms.

Television

School-age children can become over-stimulated and sometimes frightened by what they see on television, videos or computer games, and this will affect their quantity and quality of sleep. A poll of 1,300 families found that seven in 10 children have their own television while six in 10 have a games console. Research shows that children with a television in their bedroom sleep less than those who don't have one and their behaviour is affected, including their schoolwork. The simple advice is: don't put a television in your child's bedroom.

Stress and problems at school

Despite having a busy and tiring day, some school-age children may still be reluctant to go to bed at their allotted time. If this is true of your child, have you considered the possibility that she may be worried about something that is school-related? Perhaps she heard something in the school playground that worried her. Is she being teased? Or bullied? Is she worrying about her schoolwork? Find a good time to have a little chat with her and ask her gently if there is anything on her mind.

Bear in mind, too, that just as school can be stressful, any tensions there are in the household may also make children resist going to bed, especially if there are arguments between her parents when she leaves them.

Summary

To overcome resistance to going to bed:

● Set a consistent bedtime. Give notice that bedtime is approaching and what has to be done in the remaining time. Offer choice, such as, 'Bedtime is in ten minutes. Do you want some help finishing your homework?'

● Create a set of bedtime rituals that help your child wind down. Complete them in the same order every night without rushing or changing things too much. When the routine is completed, state firmly that it is over and it is now time for sleep.

● Make it clear that your child must stay in her room when the bedtime routine is over and must not come out and disturb you. There will be times when your child is not sleepy or she doesn't fall asleep immediately every time, because children tend to do this when they are ready. If this is the case, let her entertain herself by reading or playing with her toys in her room until she feels she is ready to sleep, but impress upon her that you will not bc coming back to keep her company and that you do noe expect her to seek you out to do so.

What to do when it all goes wrong

An unwillingness to go to bed and go to sleep and stay asleep are all common problems amongst children of all ages, and they usually have their roots in a variety of causes. Here are just a few things that can induce resistance to going to bed or sleep, and some suggestions on how you can tackle them and win the battle to get your child to sleep! Below is a set of problems from raisingkids.co.uk which all concern issues with going to bed or staying in bed in the evening.

Problem: No routine

My child will just not stay in his bed. Whatever time he goes to bed he is up and down like a yo-yo all evening until we are all exhausted. Most nights he goes to bed when we do and he is obviously tired because he falls asleep immediately. What can we do?

Some children have no bedtime routine. They fall asleep any time between 7 p.m. and midnight, or even go to bed when their parents do. There is no predictable and pleasurable wind-down to take the steam out of the day. It is no surprise then that they quickly move to hyperactive behaviour and get too wound-up to sleep.

Long term, children with no sleep routine become chronically sleep-deprived, their behaviour suffers and their learning and development are detrimentally affected. If you recognize your child from this description, it's time to make a change – for your child's sake.

Solution: Introduce a bedtime routine

o First, recognize that children need regular sleep if they are to thrive. Children have natural sleep rhythms which are determined by their biology. Over-permissive parents who allow their children to determine their own bedtimes, in line with what the child *wants* rather than what she needs, are denying their child vital rest and regeneration.

o Children need boundaries – and this includes definite bedtimes. They need to feel that there is order in the world, and it makes them feel protected when their parents set boundaries and rules. When children are allowed to call the shots, they often feel uneasy that they, and not their parents, are in control.

o Make a bedtime routine pleasurable. If it is a calm and relaxing part of the day and a special, unhurried time, children will look forward to it and value it for its own sake.

Problem: Incorrect associations with falling asleep

My daughter is 15 months old and she has never fallen asleep by herself in all that time. Either my husband or I have to stay with her until she falls asleep. She is a very light sleeper and if we try to slip out before she's really asleep she wakes up and starts to cry. When will it end? How can we get her to sleep without us?

Incorrect sleep associations are among the most common sleep-related problems. Put simply, instead of associating falling asleep with being in a cot or in a bed alone, drowsy and ready to go to sleep, the child associates the process of falling asleep with other activities such as:

- Being rocked or held.
- A parent lying down alongside her.
- A parent staying in the same room with her until she falls asleep.
- Being breastfed or taking a bottle.
- Sleeping in her parents' bed or in the living room.

When children wake in the night during periods of light sleep, those with the correct sleep associations will find themselves where they expect to be (in their cot, in the dark) and will go back to sleep almost immediately. But children who have incorrect sleep associations find that, when they wake, what they associate with falling asleep (rocking, singing, breastfeeding or having their parent alongside them) is not there. These children will then cry for their parents to provide them with the stimulation they need to be able to go back to sleep.

The solution to this problem lies in substituting the correct associations of a standard bedtime routine for the incorrect ones, which should lead to the child learning to settle herself and to fall asleep within minutes. There are two approaches to solving this problem. Solution one (known as controlled crying) will bring results more quickly, but is harder work (see Chapter 5); solution two (gradual withdrawal: see below) takes more time but is less upsetting for both parent and child. However, be warned that both approaches require persistence and commitment.

Solution: Gradual withdrawal

This approach is based on the idea of slowly removing yourself from your child's room a little at a time. To do this:

o Make sure you have a regular sleep routine for setting the baby down in her cot, or older child into her bed.

o If you are used to lying down on the bed with your older child, explain that you are not going to do this any more but that you will sit on a chair next to the bed. Your toddler may object, but be firm. Stress that you will stay with her but that you will not lie down on the bed. Stay until your child has fallen asleep.

o Repeat this for the next two or three nights until your child is used to the new routine.

o Gradually move the chair further away from the cot in

When to act?

A good rule of thumb when deciding on the best way to deal with a problem is to ask yourself, 'If this goes on for another year, will I still feel it's okay?' If the answer is no, don't encourage it; it is usually more difficult to break an entrenched bad habit than to build new, good ones.

stages. Stay in each spot for the next two or three nights, working towards the door. Eventually you will have moved the chair outside the room. If your child accepts this, she will be able to fall asleep without you there.

Problem: Our child falls asleep downstairs and is then carried upstairs

I know this is wrong but we have got into the habit of letting our two-and-a-half-year-old fall asleep with us while we watch television in the evening. My husband says we have to stop doing this, but each time we take her to her bed she cries and cries until we take her downstairs.

If your child resists going to bed and makes a big fuss, as only toddlers can, it may seem like a good idea to let her fall asleep on the sofa and then, when she is fast asleep, take her to her bed.

This might not seem to be a problem; after all, she is asleep and stays in her bed for the rest of the night, so what's wrong with that? True, and while it's all very well to carry a two-year-old upstairs, do you want to be carrying a five-year-old or older child who has to go to school the next day?

Solution

O Establish a good going-to-bed routine which ends with the child in her cot or bed, ready to fall asleep.

O At first your child will probably come down several times in the evening and may become even more demanding and resistant. At this point you may feel like weakening and trying again another time. Don't: it won't get easier. If you give in after an hour it will only teach her that if she cries for long enough, you will eventually relent. Stick to your guns: it's best for her as well as best for you.

O If your child is in a cot and unable to get out, follow the controlled crying routine (see page 133–4) to set up new cues for falling asleep.

O If you are dealing with a toddler who can get out of bed and come to find you herself, a different approach is required. Return her to her bed *each and every time she comes down with no explanation, no cajoling or persuasion.* Take her back to bed without saying anything except, 'You have to go to sleep in your bed.' Say it firmly and clearly and repeat it when she protests.

O If this doesn't work, you may have to try holding the door closed for a short amount of time while she is in her room. (For more information on this approach, see Chapter 5 on night waking.)

Problem: Dad comes home at bedtime and disrupts the routine

My partner gets off work early on a Monday and comes home and plays with our son before bedtime. The problem is that it spoils the routine I have and my son finds it difficult to get to sleep after all the excitement. The next day my son fights going to bed. I think he hopes his dad will be coming to play. I love to see them playing but my son is now getting really difficult to put to bed.

Working dads may have little chance to see their children during the week, so if they are able to get home for bedtime, naturally they will want to spend some time with them. The problem is that dads often like to play games and have boisterous fun, which, of course, makes the child over-excited and reluctant to go to bed.

A knock-on effect of this may be that the following night the child will want to wait up to see if Dad will turn up again and won't want to go to bed in case he does!

Solution

◉ The primary carer should establish a routine and make sure that both parties stick to it.

◉ If Dad wants to spend time with the baby/toddler in the evening, he should simply take over from Mum and follow the established routine.

Problem: We had a routine, but now our child has started to resist it

My little boy has always been a good sleeper but in the last few weeks he fusses and fusses about going to bed. I don't think anything is upsetting him, but my husband and I are going through a bad patch. Do you think it is possible that he somehow senses what's happening?

As with many elements of raising children, it often seems that you are taking one step forward and two steps back, which is definitely the case if your child is now fighting against a well-established routine. The good news is that there is usually a reason behind this new resistance – you just need to determine what that is.

Solution:

O Ask yourself *why now*? Has something happened in the household that is making him stressed or anxious? Or is your child aged between eight and 15 months? If so, he may be experiencing separation anxiety and need more reassurance and comfort.

O Is he really tired? Are you putting him to bed before he is tired because he is napping too late and too long in the afternoon and is not sleepy in the evening? If so, shorten or drop the afternoon nap. Or could he have late sleep phase shift? (See page 108.)

O Try to make sure that your child is outsied during the day and that older children are active outdoors. The combination of fresh air and exercise will make them tired and ready for bed.

○ If your child is older, has he seen something on television before going to bed that has frightened him or is just too stimulating? As a general rule, don't allow television viewing within two hours before the time that you want your child to fall asleep.

○ Has he started eating later in the day and too soon before going to bed? If so, change the time of your evening meal. Or has he got into the habit of drinking something with caffeine in it (which includes hot chocolate) and as a consequence is he over-excited?

Problem: Our child is not tired at her normal bedtime

My four-year-old goes to bed every evening at eight o'clock, which seems right for her age. But she doesn't fall asleep for two or three hours. If we let her stay up she is chirpy and lively. The problem is that she is really difficult to wake in the morning. She is going to school in September and I worry she won't be able to get up on time. Please help.

If your child is not tired at what you regard as her normal bedtime and doesn't want to go to bed until, say, ten or eleven o'clock, it is possible that your child is undergoing 'late sleep phase shift'. Alternatively, you might be finding that your child goes to bed willingly at her usual time but she is still awake two or three hours later.

Late and early sleep phase

The natural circadian wake–sleep cycle is not 24 hours but 25 hours per day. What keeps the circadian rhythms to a 24-hour cycle are the waking, eating and sleeping routines that structure the day.

A child stays on a 24-hour cycle if she has a fixed bedtime and nap times, but if this is left unchecked there is a tendency for a child's sleep–wake time to slip later and later. This means that she gets tired later and later in the evening. When she goes to bed, she sleeps for the average number of hours for her age. The problem comes in the morning when she has to be woken up – often with difficulty. If not roused the child gets the average amount of

Signs of late sleep phase shift

Typical signs of a late sleep phase shift are:

O A child isn't sleepy until well after her usual bedtime.

O She becomes sleepy later in the evening and goes to bed without a problem.

O If not woken up in the morning, the child sleeps an average amount for her age.

O The child is very difficult to wake in the morning.

O She is grumpy or lethargic in the morning and may not feel like eating breakfast.

O If she travels to school by car, she may fall into deep sleep on the journey.

sleep for her age (if she can sleep in late and doesn't need to be up for nursery/school in the morning), but the timing of the sleep (night sleep and naps) has shifted later by a couple of hours.

This shift can occur in two different ways – early and late. The late form is more common, as the 25 hour circadian cycle tends to encourage staying up late. Those children who have late sleep phase shift become very tired and tend to end up being sleep-deprived. Very young children will be allowed to sleep later in the morning to make up for lack of sleep the night before, but school children have to wait until the weekend to catch up lost hours of sleep because they need to be up at a set time in the morning during the week. Some parents even keep their child at home occasionally to catch up on missed sleep. However, all these actions are counter-productive and in fact have the effect of further shifting the cycle into the evening.

Solution:

o Keep a sleep diary to see how much and when your child is sleeping. If she is getting enough sleep but the whole sleep–wake cycle has moved to a later time than is desirable, you need to get into a routine that is more suited to your lifestyle.

o Make sure you have a relaxing going-to-bed routine. Bring the routine closer to the time she is *actually* going to sleep (whether 10 p.m. or 11 p.m.), not the time you *want* her to go to sleep. If you have been getting agitated because she is awake for much of the evening, take the pressure off and let her stay up without any arguments.

○ Don't do anything about changing her going-to-bed time too quickly; you cannot *make* a child go to sleep. Let your child stay up until she feels tired, then put her to bed after a calming sequence of events. Then start to wake your child 15 minutes earlier than usual in the morning. Move her wake-up time forward by 15 minutes every three or four days until the original waking-up time has moved forward by 45–60 minutes.

○ Stick to the morning routine every day, *including at the weekend*. This is very important. To encourage your child to get out of bed, you could arrange a fun outing for her early on Saturday and Sunday mornings.

○ Once her waking time has shifted, move her bedtime forward by 15 minutes per night, monitoring whether or not she falls asleep within 15 minutes of going to bed. Continue doing this until the sleep cycle conforms to that of the household.

Problem: Our child keeps coming downstairs

Since my little girl moved from her cot to a bed, going to bed has been a nightmare. Despite being tired and ready to sleep, she comes downstairs with a whole raft of excuses for staying up: she wants a drink, she's scared, she wants to go to the toilet or she's forgotten to tell me something. She keeps coming down again and again until finally we relent and allow her to stay up untils she falls asleep on the sofa.

As a child moves from her cot to a bed you lose the barrier that prevents her getting out of bed and now she refuses to settle down and fall asleep.

This may not immediately appear to be a sleep problem, but it is an issue that concerns sleep. The problem here is the failure to set limits on the child's behaviour. When your child goes to bed, the rule is that she has to stay in bed. This rule has to be enforced when she breaks it by coming downstairs over and over again. By relenting after many trips downstairs, what the parents are actually doing is reinforcing not just coming down, but *repeated* trips out of bed. In effect, they have encouraged their child to persist in this behaviour.

Solution:

o If you have a routine in place but your child still won't stay in bed, tell her that there are new rules as from today: she is no longer allowed to get out of bed once you leave the room.

o When your child gets up, simply take her hand and return her to bed. Say nothing except, 'You have to stay in bed and go to sleep.'

o Repeat this as often as is necessary.

o For an easy-going, tractable child this may be enough. However, for a stronger-willed, more resistant child you may have to try stronger tactics. When you return her to her bed after repeated escape attempts, tell her that you are going to close the door and hold it closed so that she

Number of minutes the door is held closed each evening

	DAY 1	DAY 2	DAY 3	DAY 4	DAY 5	DAY 6
1ST TIME	1	2	3	4	5	10
2ND TIME	2	4	5	7	10	15
3RD TIME	3	5	7	10	15	20
REMAINING	4	6	9	13	20	25

cannot come out. When she tries to open the door, hold it closed and tell her that she must get back into bed before you will open it. *The message is: if she wants the door to be opened she must stay in her bed.*

○ Hold the door closed for one minute before going in. If she is in bed, praise her, then leave, keeping the door open. If she is not in bed, take her to her bed, remind her of the new rules and leave the room. If she gets out of bed again, this time hold the door closed for two minutes.

○ Repeat the process. On the third occasion, hold the door for three minutes and next time for four. Don't go above four minutes on the first night, but repeat this until she settles into her bed. Whenever she returns to her bed, praise her. When she stays in her bed be sure to praise her. You can use this method in conjunction with a star chart or a system of rewards. (See Chapter 5 for information on star charts.) Talk to her through the door, explaining that if she gets into bed you will open the door. Be calm but firm. This will be difficult for you and your child and you will both need some time to get used to the new approach.

o On the second night, hold the door for a little longer and do the same again on subsequent days. Use the schedule outlined opposite. This solution will be difficult to enforce if you have a strong-willed toddler, so undertake this approach only if you think you can follow through on it.

Holding the door closed while your child is crying on the other side of it is very hard to do. Remember, though, that this will not do any psychological damage to your child and you are not doing this to punish her, but to teach her that having the door open is within her control. With a graduated approach your child will learn that she is not locked in; that you will open the door, *but that she can also open it simply by returning to bed.*

Depending on how long the habit of getting out of bed has been established, most children will respond to this approach within 10 days.

Problem: Our 10-year-old never sleeps in her own room

What do you do with a 10-year-old who has never gone to sleep in her own room since the family moved house five years before? This is a problem raisingkids.co.uk received from a frantic parent and an example of how sleeping problems can get out of hand.

My 10-year-old daughter has never gone to sleep in her own room since we moved house five years ago. Since then, she only sleeps there if a friend stays, or if I stay with her until she falls asleep. If she wakes up in the night, she comes and calls me to get into her bed or lies down on the floor in our bedroom. She regularly sleeps on the floor of her 14-year-old sister's room (although my eldest gets very fed up with it). When we first moved house it was a somewhat traumatic time for her, but now she seems to be otherwise happy and settled.

A short-term problem?

Parents of toddlers who won't sleep alone, or who come into their parents' room during the night, may comfort themselves with the thought that they 'will grow out of it'. Well, not necessarily so, as another mother revealed to raisingkids.co.uk:

'My son has seldom slept through the night. My husband and I would bring him into our bed or go to sleep in his bed, so everyone could get some rest. Now I realize that this was a huge mistake! I have just given birth to my second child and our son wakes at least three times a night screaming and crying for me to sleep with him. This is impossible, because of the nightly feeding schedule of my newborn. I feel horrible because I know I have created this situation and my entire family is paying for it, especially my son.'

Solution

○ As this girl was older, talking to her was a major part of the solution. The mother had to get her daughter to 'own the problem' and involve her in finding the solution. She needed to explain that the whole family found her behaviour a nuisance and that it was no longer okay for her to do this. It was important for the mother to get her daughter to agree that she would like to be able to sleep all night alone, in her own bedroom.

○ In this situation it is a good idea to ask the child for her suggestions for ways in which she could break the habit and to fix a date by which she will have solved the problem. Make a list of her ideas and perhaps then discuss each one and whether they are plausible.

○ Agree that when she comes to your bedroom (or anyone else's) she can't stay there and must go back to her own bed. If necessary, take her back to her room yourself, even though this will mean several broken nights for you.

○ Accommodate her requests for ways in which you can make this change easier for her (within reason!), such as leaving lights on low, leaving your bedroom door open, and so on, but get her to agree that she will stay in her own room if these things are done.

○ Promise her a (big) reward when she overcomes her difficulties.

Don't forget

O There is a number of reasons why children resist going to bed, which include irregular sleep patterns, incorrect sleep associations and late sleep phase shift.

O There are several strategies to get your child into going to bed without any fuss but they do require persistence and consistency.

O The longer your child has refused to settle at night, the longer it will take to change her habit.

O When you are tempted to move away from your routine, ask yourself, 'Will it be okay if this habit goes on for months, or even years?'

Waking in the night

If your toddler is still keeping you up at night, don't think that you are alone in this: up to 30 per cent of under-threes regularly wake in the night, and 33 per cent of them are taken into their parents' bed when they do.

Any issues about settling a child down for the night pale into insignificance when compared to problems that arise *during* the night. Most parents can cope with early evening traumas because, difficult though they may be, the children are usually settled by a reasonable hour and so the process does not cut into the adults' own sleep time. Persistent night-time waking, however, is another matter, especially if it goes on for months, because by then parents will be suffering from chronic sleep deprivation.

Parents may start off intending that their child sleeps in his own bed throughout the night, but they might find their resolve weakens as their toddler pads into their bedroom for what seems like the hundredth time in one night. It is no wonder that many parents relent at this point and, desperate for a good night's sleep, decide the best solution is to bring their child into bed with them.

But stop there. Yes, this can be a quick fix to the problem, but it won't solve the problem. In fact, giving in after many visits will inadvertently encourage his *repeated* visits. Once your child is in the habit of sleeping in your bed, getting him back to his own bed will take a lot of effort and time.

One of the most important aspects of parenting, and in particular of sleep training, is consistency. Unless your child is ill or upset about something important, it is vital that you

Stand firm!

If you want your child to sleep in his own bed during the night, don't give in to the temptation to bring him into yours: you will only be creating another problem.

stick to your routine, both for going to bed and for dealing with night-time waking.

Going to sleep and staying asleep

Partial waking

All sleepers of all ages habitually surface from deep sleep at various times of the night. Most will simply resettle themselves and are not even conscious of having been partially awake. Night-time sleeping problems occur when the sleeper moves from being partially awake to being fully awake and cannot go back to sleep. With adults this is usually because there is something on their mind which surfaces to consciousness during partial arousal. This underlying worry or anxiety will force them into complete wakefulness.

In children there are four common circumstances that are associated with night waking:

o Night feeding. Baby wakes and wants to be fed. This is not a sleep issue; it is perfectly natural behaviour in the first three months (when night feeding is to be expected). Night

Medical causes of waking at night

Sometimes a child may wake at night because he is feeling unwell or is in pain or discomfort. You should suspect a medical cause for night waking if:

○ Your baby awakens with sudden, colicky-type abdominal pains. You will recognize from his crying that he is in pain.

○ A good sleeper suddenly becomes a restless sleeper.

○ There are other signs or symptoms of illness, such as a temperature, lethargy or lack of appetite.

○ Your baby cries inconsolably.

○ Your intuition tells you that something is wrong.

Below is a list of some of the more common causes of night waking. Some are difficult to detect because they are not as obvious as other prime suspects, such as ear infections, teething or urinary-tract infections.

1 Ear infections

Babies with ear infections may rub their ear fretfully and cry extensively with the pain. Look on the cot sheets by the baby's head for specks of a discharge from the ear. If you spot any of these signs, consult a doctor as soon as possible.

2 Gastroesophageal reflux (GER)

When a baby lies flat, irritating stomach acids are regurgitated into the oesophagus, causing a pain that adults call 'heartburn'. GER or, as it most commonly referred to, reflux can often be successfully treated with smaller, more frequent feeds, raising the head of the cot by 30 degrees or, in some cases, putting the baby to sleep upright in a pushchair or car seat.

If the problem is severe, you should consult your doctor.

3 Food allergies

You should suspect a food allergy is the problem if your baby is restless most of the night and is generally gassy. Some babies will also display very red cheeks and a runny nose and may be sick.

Some allergies can have serious effects on a child, so if your child is sick and starts to have problems breathing after eating something, call an ambulance immediately. Such reactions can be a sign of a severe allergy which could be triggering an anaphylactic attack.

4 Threadworms

A toddler or older child who is waking up with scratch marks around the anus may have threadworms. Look for tiny, white, thread-like worms around his anus or in his bowel movements. Check other members of the family, too, because threadworms are very easily spread. The condition is a little more obvious in older children, who may experience pain on urinating and might wake up in the night needing to go to the toilet.

feeding becomes an issue that needs to be addressed when it occurs in older babies who are capable of sleeping for four or five hours without being fed.

○ Inappropriate sleep associations. The child wakes in his cot and is alone but he is used to falling asleep with a parent with him. The only way he can get back to sleep is if one of his parents comes to help him. This is known as an inappropriate sleep association, where the child can fall asleep only if certain conditions are met. This commonly occurs when a baby is rocked, cuddled or fed until he falls asleep. In older children it might be because the parent stays with them until they sleep or they stay up with the family and fall asleep outside their cot.

○ Increased mobility at night. An older child who has moved from a cot into a bed may wake in the night and find that he is now able to get out of bed. Even a child who is used to going to sleep alone may wake up and become fearful in the dark, decide to get out of bed and go into his parents' bedroom for reassurance.

○ Medical or emotional reason. The child might wake up for medical (see pages 120–1) or emotional reasons.

Babies under three months

In the first few months, young babies will wake several times during the night in order to be fed. Never leave a baby under the age of six weeks to cry for any length of time. Babies have a tiny stomach and their mother's milk is digested very rapidly, they get hungry frequently and crying is their only way of letting their mother know. If a baby's stimulus for hunger could not easily arouse him and his sleep state was so deep that he could not communicate his needs, his survival would be jeopardized. Crying – which elicits strong responses in mothers – is a baby's most effective means of communicating what it is that hc wants.

So in these first few months the baby's needs are paramount. However, even at this early stage there is something that parents can do to encourage their baby into good sleeping habits, while still being totally responsive to his needs.

How you and your baby can get the best night's sleep

○ Wake your baby for a late night feed before you go to bed yourself.

○ If he wakes and whimpers, chances are he will fall asleep again, so wait a minute or two bcforc you go to him. If it is a full blown 'Come now, I'm hungry!' cry, go to him as soon as the crying begins. Don't wait for him to cry himself back to sleep, as he will soon wake again, which iust means that he will interrupt your sleep one more time.

○ Wrap him up warmly (but not too hot so that he overheats), so that temperature drops at night won't wake him.

○ When he cries, respond quickly, but view this as a time for changing and feeding only. To encourage the idea that night-time is for sleeping, don't provide any unnecessary stimulation, such as talking or playing, and keep the lights dim, if they have to be on at all.

○ Make night feeds and changes as short as possible by having everything ready and to hand.

○ Once baby has been fed, put him back into his cot. He is likely to fall asleep immediately, so don't hold him or rock him until he falls asleep.

Babies over three months

At three to four months, when the sleep–wake cycle is developing, you can start to encourage your baby to sleep longer at night. Begin by feeding him when you go to bed between 10 p.m. and 11 p.m. and you may find that he sleeps until 4 a.m. or 5 a.m. At this point your baby will have given up one of his night feeds, but there is no reason to make up for it by giving him extra formula at night: he doesn't need it and it won't make him sleep longer.

All babies have several periods of lighter sleep during the night and you might hear them cry or whimper. How you react to these arousal periods is critical for establishing good sleeping habits. If you know that your baby can sleep through until early morning, don't be too quick to go to him when he stirs in the night. Wait a few minutes and see if he will go back to sleep by himself.

It's important to recognize that babies aren't always awake when they *sound* like they are. Babies can stir or grizzle or even cry loudly during light sleep. If you imme- diately rush to his side, pick him up, give him something to drink or even play with him, guess what happens at the next period of wakefulness? Chances are that he will

It's your choice

Some parents prefer to respond to what they interpret as their child's need for comfort and not leave him to settle himself. They would rather live with interruptions to their own sleep than endure their baby's cries. This is most common amongst new parents, who are anxious that something is wrong and want to reassure themselves that their baby is okay.

Other parents believe that it's important to help their child to learn to sleep by himself. They know that a few nights of tears during the learning process are balanced by the longer-term benefit of better sleep for the whole family. Choosing this approach means developing an ability to understand your child's cries. Mothers learn to distinguish between a child's cry of distress and crying because of hunger, boredom or being tired or uncomfortable.

Listen carefully to your baby's cries. Is he crying because he is tired? Irritable? Wants some company? Or is he in pain? There is a difference between the cries he makes when he is half asleep and those he makes when he is fully awake. As he gets older you will learn to distinguish between his various cries and interpret his needs from them. Unless you think he is actually in pain, take a little time before going to him. He may just as easily go back to sleep.

become wide awake and cry for the attention he got the last time he woke up. Your baby is learning to associate waking up in the night and falling asleep again with other activities – all of which require you to be there.

Pre-school children

Issues of night-waking are also very common among toddlers. In the second year of their life many children become strong-willed and independent-minded. If they wake in the night and want company, their cries will often escalate and becoming more insistent – and more difficult to ignore.

This is also the age at which their imagination is developing and they will have ideas and fantasies that make them fearful and upset. An imaginative child who wakes alone, in the dark and in a silent house might worry about monsters, ghosts and other scary things that go bump in the night. Small wonder, then, that at these times he looks for reassurance from his parents and goes to their bedroom.

Other things that might make a toddler unsettled include tensions within the household, changes in family circumstances – such as moving house or the arrival of a new sibling – starting nursery or being left with a new carer. Daytime anxieties can be buried while he is busy and occupied, but they often surface in the small hours of the morning when he has nothing to distract him.

So what do you do when your child appears at your bedside for the fourth or fifth time in one night? The easy solution might be to let your child settle down in bed with

On the move

One of the major sleep-related developments during the first five years of a child's life is the move from a cot to a bed. Once your child is able to get out of his bed the problems can really begin, because now it is easy for him to come to the living room in the early evening or to your bedroom during the night.

It helps if your child is already in the habit of falling asleep alone in his cot, in his room, well before he moves into a bed. Be warned, though, that this in itself won't stop night-time wandering. Even children who had settled happily in their cots may now start to get out of bed in the night – sometimes just because they can!

you, but a word of warning on this: unless you are prepared to put up with it for longer than one or two nights, don't do it. If you give in on this, you are merely introducing another set of sleep associations – 'being in Mummy's bed'. What then happens is that next time he wakes in the night, the only way to get back to sleep is to be 'in Mummy's bed'.

So the key to solving this problem, and nipping it in the bud, is to start as you mean to go on. The first time your child comes to your bed, get up and soothe him (either in or out of your bed), but once he is calm, tell him that it's time to go back to his own bed. Quietly take him back to his own room and put him into his bed, tuck him in, say goodnight and leave. Don't give him something to drink or be sucked into singing him a lullaby or reading him a story; don't talk or explain why you're taking him back to bed, just say: 'You must sleep in your own bed now.'

Children of school age

The persistent night-waking of pre-school-age children will slowly decline as they move towards the age of five, at which point even those children who were regular wakers or visitors to their parents' bed will have settled into their own night-time routine.

When they start school the majority of children will be sleeping a whole night without interruption in their own room. There will be a few occasions on which children come into their parents' room in the night, but this should now be the exception rather than the rule. Usually this will happen because they are unwell, or perhaps because there is a big change taking place in their life that they are worried about.

If parents are aware that their children are lying awake at night, they should consider the possibility that they are worried about something. If your child comes into your room in the night saying he has had a bad dream or 'can't stop thinking', make a time the next day to talk about it. Just talking about it and reassuring him that all is well might just be enough to stop his waking at night.

Don't forget that children of this age are becoming very aware of what is happening around them and they will pick up on problems at home. If a child's parents have a difficult relationship, for example, he may make excuses to stay up at night just so that he can prevent his parents arguing.

As children grow older they are more likely to encounter problems outside the home which will cause them additional stress or worry. They may be concerned about their schoolwork or their friendships, or scared because they are being teased or bullied in class.

For children moving towards their teens, life becomes yet more complex and worrying as they start to think about some of the 'bigger' questions in life. They may be anxious about their future, or even the future of the world. This is also the age at which children become aware of illness and death and begin to understand what they mean, often because they might experience the loss of close family members during this time. These experiences can cause sensitive and emotional children to lie awake at night, mulling them over. Worries about secondary school, the onset of adolescent body changes and crises of confidence are all typical issues for pre-adolescents.

These days life is very busy for the typical school child. There is homework to do in the evening, favourite television programmes to watch, extra-curricular activities to pursue, friends to speak to on the phone or send texts to, the latest music to listen to and DVDs to watch (all too often in their bedrooms).

This makes for a stimulating and exciting day – not the right circumstances for winding down for bed. Some of this stimulation might linger in the child's mind and keep him awake. Do make sure that before your child goes to bed he has some quiet time to relax and wind down. Don't let him watch frightening programmes on television close to his bedtime, and ban television watching in his bedroom before going to sleep (or, better still, remove the television from his room).

What to do when things go wrong

Problem: Baby cries and won't settle until I go in to him

By the time a child is five or six months old, conditions are favourable for both parents and their baby to get a reasonable night of uninterrupted sleep. So why do some babies still wake several times in the night?

Those babies who do not wake through the night are able to move alone through the transition from deep sleep to lighter sleep, a process often referred to as 'self-soothing'. This expression implies the baby is distressed and, because he is unable to get a parent to respond, is forced to soothe himself. However, this is not a correct reading of what is happening: there is no evidence to suggest that a baby is distressed when he is partially awake. When these self-soothing babies find themselves in a state of partial arousal, instead of coming to a full awakening they simply slip back into sleep.

Partial awakening during sleep is normal, and unaided return to sleep is also normal. Billions of sleepers do it every night. Babies who become alert at this stage are missing one of the 'props' they rely on to settle themselves back to sleep, such as a toy, a comfort blanket, a dummy or, more usually, a parent to hold, rock or otherwise soothe them. These babies have incorrect sleep associations, so in the absence of their props they are forced to cry out to their parents to come and provide them.

The longer this habit has been established, the more difficult it is to break. So if your intention is to have your child sleep in his own bed throughout the night, now is the time to start.

When a baby with incorrect sleep associations wakes and cries in the night, look for the solution to the problem, not in the night, but in the early evening when he is settled down to sleep. This is the time at which sleep associations are generally formed. Consult Chapter 4 on ways to change the incorrect associations and substitute them with a well-oiled sleep routine that tells the baby that it's time to go to sleep.

Once he settles in his cot alone and falls asleep without his 'props', it will be easier to tackle his night-time waking. It may well be that once he gets into an early evening bedtime routine and settles himself to sleep alone, the night-waking stops by itself. If he continues to wake at night, though, try one of the two tactics outlined on the next few pages: controlled crying or gradual withdrawal.

Solution 1: Controlled crying

o The first step is to separate the process of falling asleep from the incorrect sleep associations that have built up. Controlled crying is a sleep-training method which requires that you listen to your baby crying without going in to comfort him. Some parents find this approach very difficult, and if you don't think you can follow through with this, try the alternative solution of gradual withdrawal instead (see pages 102–3).

o If you don't already have a clear bedtime routine, now is the time to start one (see Chapter 4). When you have finished the routine, say goodnight and leave the room. This is the first hurdle, as your child is used to you staying with him until he falls asleep.

o If your baby cries when you leave the room, don't go back in. Stay outside the door for five minutes while he is crying. Don't let him see you or hear you. Time yourself, because it will seem longer.

o If your baby is still crying after five minutes, return to the room but don't interact with him. Avoid eye contact and don't speak. Let him see you, put your hand on his tummy gently to calm him down and then, when he is settled, leave the room again, quietly saying 'goodnight'.

o If your baby starts to cry again, repeat the process but this time wait for eight minutes. If he hasn't settled after eight minutes, go in to him.

o The third time you return, do so after 12 minutes. If he still doesn't settle, repeat this process with 12-minute waits each time until he falls asleep. On the first night, don't wait for more than 12 minutes for the crying to stop.

o On the second night, repeat the procedure, staying outside the door for a little longer this time. Start with a 10-minute wait on the first occasion, increasing this to 15 minutes on the second and 20 minutes on the third. Don't go above a 20-minute wait on the second night.

o On the third night, increase the start time to 15 minutes and add five minutes each time you return.

Your baby is not crying because he is hurt, hungry or in pain, but because his expectations are dashed. This is the only way he can communicate his feelings. Leaving him to cry for a short time will not cause him any psychological or emotional harm.

The table below sets out the recommended timings for using the controlled-crying technique over a period of six days. The upper limit on waiting time is 45 minutes, which will be very difficult for most parents. If the situation has not improved after six days, follow the Day 6 routine.

Controlled-crying timings

	DAY 1	DAY 2	DAY 3	DAY 4	DAY 5	DAY 6
1ST CHECK	5	10	15	20	25	30
2ND CHECK	8	15	18	23	28	35
3RD CHECK	12	20	24	25	30	40
REMAINING CHECKS	12	20	24	25	35	45

Controlled crying is a sleep-training method many parents will find difficult. It may be a struggle at first and hard for you to listen to your child crying, but remember that he is not being harmed by what you are doing. Your child is perfectly capable of sleeping through the night without you, and the sooner you get him into a good sleep routine, the better.

After a few days, your baby should get the message and learn how to sleep without your presence. The younger the child, the quicker he will respond to this programme, but be flexible and trust your instincts. An older child with a more firmly established habit will probably take a little longer to teach.

Because controlled crying can be emotionally tough for parents, don't start it unless you are confident that you can see it through to the end. If you decide after a couple of days that you can't stand it any more and relent, what your child will learn is that *prolonged* crying pays off and it will be more difficult to break this habit at a later date.

However, don't let a very young baby cry for more than 20 minutes and do take into account any special circumstances that might be causing him to wake, such as teething, illness or changes in routines. If any of these apply, stop the sleep training and start again when he is well enough. Equally, if your baby is very clingy during waking hours it may be that he is experiencing separation anxiety and so will easily become distraught. If this is the case, modify the schedule and keep the intervals shorter or wait until he seems less clingy during the day.

Start as you mean to go on

Try to get into good sleeping habits before the onset of the attachment stage. If you start sleep training from three months, by six months your baby should be able to settle down in the early evening with little fuss.

The advantage of the controlled-crying method is that it reassures your baby that you are still there and have not abandoned him. The alternative – leaving him to cry himself to sleep in one long crying bout – is not advisable, because it may leave your baby feeling bereft and abandoned.

Solution 2: Gradual withdrawal

If you find it difficult or impossible to let your baby cry as long as is necessary with the controlled-crying technique, you could try slowing weaning him off your presence by the gradual withdrawal process. To recap, in the beginning you should sit on a chair by the cot, but don't talk to your baby or cuddle him. After two days move the chair nearer to the door and away from the cot. Every two days move a little further away until you are outside the door, at which point he will be able to go back to sleep without you.

Problem: Breastfeeding in the night

Most babies will have given up their night feed by the age of five or six months, but some babies persist in waking for a feed, sometimes several times a night. Below is a cry for help that we received at raisingkids.co.uk, from a mother whose child was totally reliant upon breastfeeding to fall asleep.

My baby is six months old and the night-waking has me completely exhausted. He may wake up several times to feed either a little or a lot. Please help!

There were two possible reasons why this baby was waking up at night to be fed. When his mother says he sometimes feeds a lot, that implies that he is hungry and is in the habit of waking in the night to feed. After the age of three or four months most babies have given up their night feed, so this behaviour is unusual.

When she says that sometimes he feeds only a little, that suggests he associates falling back to sleep with sucking. Depending on the reason for the waking, the solution to the problem differs.

Habit

If a baby sucks hungrily and takes the equivalent of a full feed, it is clear that he is waking up for the food. This can be confirmed in the morning by checking his nappy. After several 'full' feeds his nappy will be soaking wet.

Night-feeders also wake in the night for other, connected, reasons: if they drink a lot they may be wet and uncomfortable and so they want a nappy change. Also, their digestion is being stimulated during the night when it should be shut down, which could be giving them some physical discomfort.

The fact that the baby is consuming a lot of milk in the night doesn't necessarily mean that he is hungry. Most babies don't have a night feed at six months and he will not be harmed if the night feeds are cut out. Sometimes a baby 'learns' to be hungry at certain times and an infant who has several feeds during the night can often be fitting his sleep around his feeds, just as he does during the day with his naps. This has the effect of undermining the natural day–night sleep–wake cycle.

Solution: Decrease and then cut out night-time feeds

The aim is to wean the baby slowly off the breast or the bottle at night by reducing the amount of liquid consumed at night. Don't make your baby go cold turkey and just stop feeding him at night completely, as this will be too hard for him to cope with. Do it slowly, and once you have decreased the amount of feeds taken at night, the next step is to look at and change any incorrect associations that he might have.

○ If you are bottle-feeding, reduce the amount by 28ml per feed. If breastfeeding, shorten each feed by a few minutes by removing the baby from the breast.

○ Put the baby back into the cot when he is still awake and leave the room. If he falls asleep while feeding, or if you have been in the habit of staying with him until he falls asleep, do as you usually do. The aim at this stage is just to reduce the amount of food he is taking.

● If he wakes within two hours, don't feed him again; he may appear hungry, but he does not need nourishment. If he becomes upset, comfort him without picking him up, if possible. However, if he becomes distraught because you won't pick him up, then pick him up. The emphasis at this time should be on reducing the amount of milk he drinks.

● Keep the feeds at least two hours apart on the first night. Increase the gap between feeds by twenty minutes on the following night and by an additional half hour each night after that. At the same time, continue to decrease the amount of formula or juice in the bottle or restrict the amount of time spent breastfeeding.

● Your baby may still wake at night even after he has been weaned off the nourishment, so you may need to look at his sleep associations and change these in order to help him sleep though the night.

Incorrect associations

If the baby wakes for a feed in the night but sucks only for a minute or two before falling asleep, what he wants is the breast or the sucking sensation, rather than the nourishment. In this case you can safely assume that the baby's problem is his dependence on nursing in order to fall asleep. The solution to this is to train him to fall asleep without nursing.

Solution: Change sleep associations

○ Nurse your baby as usual before you put him to bed, but take him off the breast before he falls asleep. Babies of a certain temperament will remain sleepy and mellow after being moved into their cots and will fall asleep relatively easily. More intense children can become very annoyed when they find themselves alone in their cots instead of nestled in your arms.

○ If your baby continues to cry once you have put him in his cot, the problem is best treated using the controlled-crying technique. It might be a good idea to get your partner to help out in this case, as the baby's crying may cause you to lactate and if he smells the milk on you it is likely that he might become more distressed at being denied the breast.

○ If you're not keen on sleep training him yet, you could try introducing a dummy as a compromise; it will accommodate your baby's urge to suck, but remove the need for you to nurse.

Problem: Wakes in the night and calls out

As babies grow into toddlers their desire to assert their independence becomes very pronounced. 'No' becomes a favourite word and when toddlers don't get what they want they tend to throw a tantrum and cry. This behaviour is difficult to cope with during the day and adds extra pressure if it happens when the child wakes at night, as this cry for help to raisingkids.co.uk shows:

My one-year-old has started waking several times in the night and calling out for us. We have tried just waiting, but he gets really het up and shouts even louder. I am worried that when he moves to a bed he'll be out and about in the night. How can I break this habit before it breaks me?

Solution: Comfort without interaction

O When he first cries out, wait a while before going in to him rather than hurrying to his bedside. Listen to his cry and make a judgement from this as to whether or not he is awake or still partially asleep. If he is left undisturbed, he may simply go back to sleep.

O If the crying becomes loud and insistent – as it can do during the 'terrible twos' (and threes) – something will have to be done to prevent him waking other members of the family who have school or work the next day.

O Go to his room and soothe him back to sleep using *just your presence.* Don't get drawn into any interaction with him by talking to him, fetching him a glass of water, taking him to the toilet and so on. Don't lie down with him until he falls asleep, either. Your aim is to reassure him that he is safe, then quickly return to your own bed, leaving him to fall asleep again in his bed.

O If he carries on crying, there are only two options: tough it out with controlled crying (see page 132) or use the more softly-softly gradual-withdrawal approach (see pages 102–3).

Problem: Keeps coming to parents' bedroom

As children get older they are often prey to fears which seem more vivid at night, so it is not unusual for children who wake up in the dark to feel afraid and to want comfort, which they then seek in their parents' bedroom. Here is a very common sleep problem sent in to raisingkids.co.uk by an exhausted parent:

Our four-year-old has started waking up to 10 times a night and coming into our bedroom which, as you can imagine, is taking its toll on us both mentally and physically. We always put him straight back into his bed, but he cries and keeps coming back into our room until we sit with him. He'd love us to lie with him in whichever bed we choose, but we've managed to avoid that so far and just sit next to him until he (quite quickly) drops off.

This is not a problem that has been created by incorrect sleep associations, but stems from the fact that something is happening during the night that is causing the child to wake up and cry out.

He could be scared or anxious about something and when he wakes up and finds himself alone in the dark, his fears grow. He may be frightened by something he has read, seen or been told and his imagination is doing the rest.

There is a number of approaches you can adopt to deal with this problem, ranging from tough (controlled crying) to accepting the inevitable and allowing him to sleep in his parents' room or bed. The solution you choose depends on your family's circumstances, the child's temperament, the mother's persistence and the parents' sleep requirements. Bearing this in mind, here are four different solutions for this problem.

Solution 1: Rapid return to bed

● When he comes to your room in the night, don't take him back immediately. If he is upset, give him a short cuddle in your bed until he is calm. If you believe that your child is genuinely frightened in the dark, reassure him that there are no monsters and that you, as his parents, will always make sure that he is safe. Don't dismiss his fears, but remember too that night is not the time for long-drawn-out conversations.

● Don't let him fall asleep in your bed. Once he is calm, say, 'Now you have to sleep in your own bed,' and take him back. Don't interact with him.

● The next step is critical: *don't stay with him until he falls asleep.* Often the problem is not that the child comes to his parents' room, but that when they take him back they stay with him until he falls asleep. In these situations it is the parent who has created an association of sitting with him until he falls asleep in the middle of the night. Your aim is to get him to fall asleep *without you*; then there will be no reason for him to come and get you in the middle of the night when he wakes.

○ Don't change your mind. If he keeps on coming back and wears you down until you give in, you have simply taught him that if he persists for long enough – and in this example 10 times a night is a very persistent child – you will relent. You have reinforced his determination.

○ If when you return him to bed he starts to cry but stays in bed, use the techniques of controlled crying outlined on page 134.

○ If he won't stay in bed but follows you out of his room, you may have to use the techniques described in Chapter 4 (see pages 111–13) and hold the door closed for limited amounts of time so that he cannot leave the room. Don't do this if your child is genuinely afraid. His fears, however fanciful they appear to adults, are real and what he needs is reassurance. You will know from the character of his crying if he is afraid. Suggest to him that you leave on a landing light or a nightlight. Close any open door or windows that are casting shadows into his room. Leave his door open and your door too. Do whatever it takes to calm him down and give him confidence to go back to sleep.

This approach is tough and could take up to 10 days to have an effect, so be sure that you can follow through with it, and be prepared to sacrifice a few nights' sleep for the sake of months of unbroken sleep in the future. If he starts to cry you may worry that he will wake other members of the household: if they are good sleepers they are likely to sleep through the commotion, but if he is sharing a room with a sibling, try to move the other child to another room, if possible, while you resolve this problem.

Solution 2: Gradual withdrawal

If your child is very determined, you may find it difficult or impossible to keep returning him to his bed, listening to his crying or holding the door closed. If this rings true for you, gradual withdrawal is a more gentle approach that might suit you better.

○ When you return your child to bed, don't sit by the bed, but in a chair a little distance away. Over the following nights gradually move the chair further away from the bed and closer to the door. The idea is that eventually you should be able to return him to his bed and leave immediately.

○ Another version of gradual withdrawal gives him a little of what he wants – your presence – but allows you to have a decent night's rest for most, if not all, of the night. Tell him that you will put a mattress on the floor of your bedroom and that he can sleep there if he wakes up in the night, but that he cannot come into your bed nor wake you up (although you will almost certainly wake up when you hear him coming). This way you will have a less broken night and he will be in your company, but not in your bed. and it also means that you are likely to be disturbed only once. Over a number of days (don't rush it) move the mattress closer to your bedroom door and then onto the landing. It is unlikely that he will rouse himself from his bed merely to sleep on the landing.

Solution 3: Reward charts

O If you prefer less stick and more carrot, you could try to get your child to change his bedtime habits by rewarding him for any new habits he displays. (Bear in mind that this tactic will work only with two-year-olds and older children who understand the concept of rewards for good behaviour.)

O Make a star chart for a week at a time.

O Agree a reward that your child will receive if he stays in his bed overnight without getting out for a week. *It should be something he really wants.*

O When he comes to your bed in the night, take him back to his own bed. Without interacting with him, put him into his bed, tuck him in and leave. He will get a star if he stays in bed and allows you to leave. Next morning, give him lots of praise for staying in his bed and give him the star to stick on the chart.

O Once you have enabled him to sleep without your presence he will no longer wake to come and get you but fall asleep again alone. If he does this, at the end of the week give him his reward. If he continues to come to your bedroom but only wants you to put him back into bed, start a star chart to reward staying in bed.

O If you have a partner they should be aware of the system so that they can help you and stick to the rules.

Solution 4: Wait for him to grow out of it

Some parents who are concerned that their child is fearful in the night may opt for a more relaxed route and might happily allow their child to sleep in their bed. It's the parents' choice as to when they decide to bring their child into their bed, but it may not be the parents' choice as to when he leaves!

If you can sleep anywhere and don't mind sharing your bed with a sprawling, wriggling toddler, rest assured he will probably grow out of this behaviour in time. Think ahead, though: if you have another baby, will you be able to cope with two children in your bed? It is an indisputable fact that your toddler will not want to be forced out of your bed to make way for a new baby. The SIDS recommendation is that you don't sleep with a toddler and a baby in the same bed.

Finally, for the sake of marital harmony, you need to be sure that your partner feels the same about co-sleeping. Many couples reach a stage where the child is sleeping in the mother's bed and the father in the child's bed...

Problem: Waking in the night full of energy

Another common problem is the baby who is just so interested in what is going on in the world, during both the day and night, that he doesn't seem able to switch off for the whole night. He may be exhausted at bedtime, but he will be back in exploring mode in the early hours.

My baby son is 14 months old. For the last week now he's been waking up in the middle of the night and when he does he is wide awake, wanting to play and full of energy. I simply can't get him to go back to sleep. Please help me!

Solution: Explain the distinction between day and night

O One way to solve this problem is to make very clear to your child the distinction between daytime and night-time, reinforcing the message that night-time is for sleeping.

O At the end of the going-to-bed routine, take the child through the house to say goodnight to *everything* that he associates with his daytime life: goodnight toys, goodnight television, goodnight kitchen and so on. Take your time over this to emphasize the importance of night and sleeping.

O Tell him that *everything* stays quiet and still during the night including, of course, Mummy, Daddy, all his toys and himself.

O Explain that when the daytime comes – then, but not before – everything wakes up.

O If your child is of an age where he can understand the concept, you could buy a lamp that switches on when day-light comes or a special clock that tells 'getting up time'. On the clock face is a rabbit which 'goes to sleep' when the clock is set and wakes up at the time you set the alarm. The alarm can be turned off. At your child's waking-up time the rabbit 'wakes up' and so the child can tell by looking at the clock if it is 'waking time' and if he can get up.

Of all the issues to do with sleep, persistent night-waking must be one of the most stressful for parents. There is a number of solutions that work, but some require a tougher approach and commitment. It's not only parents who suffer if their child wakes at night – he is not getting the kind of nourishing sleep he needs if it is persistently interrupted.

Don't forget

O All children wake in the night. The majority go back to sleep unaided.

O Very young babies wake and cry to be fed. Always respond to their cries.

O Children who fall asleep in the early evening with incorrect sleep associations will need the same associations in the middle of the night and so will cry for their parents to provide them.

O From six months most babies are sleeping for a long stretch in the night. Babies who are not doing so can be encouraged to.

O Once a child moves from his cot to a bed, expect that there might be nights when he comes into your bed.

O If a child is not upset or in pain when he comes to your room repeatedly in the night, use the strategy of rapid return to bed.

O To deter a child from calling for you in the night, try controlled crying, but do it only if you can carry it through.

O For a softer but slower sleep-training approach, try gradual withdrawal as an alternative.

O If you want your child to sleep in his bed in the night, don't take him into yours!

Other sleep problems

Along with problems of getting to sleep, staying asleep and getting up early in the morning, parents may also witness other issues affecting their child's sleep. In fact, at some stage in their life, about 40 per cent of children will have a sleep problem which their parents will consider a significant concern.

Children with a learning disability, a chronic physical illness such as asthma, or a psychiatric disorder such as attention deficit hyperactivity disorder (ADHD), are particularly prone to problems with sleep. The National Sleep Foundation (NSF) in the USA conducted a *Sleep in America* poll, in 2004, which revealed that around 69 per cent of children under 10 experience some type of sleep problem.

Nightmares

Most children have at least one nightmare during childhood and, according to NSF's 2004 *Sleep in America* poll, 3 per cent of pre-school and school-age children experience frequent nightmares.

Nightmares are frightening dreams which cause a child to wake up in fear. They occur during REM sleep, usually in the later part of the night. Older children may quickly go back to sleep, but infants and toddlers will often cry out and, if they are able get out of bed, will head straight for their parents' bedroom. Nightmares are usually related to anxiety and stress, but frequent nightmares may stem from images that stay in their mind after hearing a scary story or seeing a violent television show or film. Often the child will remember these scary dreams and will be able to tell you about them on waking or the next day.

At different ages children react differently to their nightmares. Their nightmares can begin as early as one or two years of age and infants will cry and scream until someone comforts them. Toddlers' bad dreams are most often about being apart from their parents, while pre-schoolers dream about monsters or scary creatures. Frightened toddlers will usually scream or head to their parents' bedroom for comfort. Older children will usually go back to sleep without waking their parents, having dreamed about death or coming face to face with real dangers.

Through the toddler and pre-school years, children develop an elaborate imagination which generally peaks at about four or five years of age. While this new imagination sparks wonderfully creative play during the day, it can also bring scary dreams or fears at night. A pre-schooler won't yet be able to distinguish between reality and fantasy, so the nightmares will seem very real to her.

Sometimes these ideas stem from something they have read in a book or seen on television. If the nightmares persist, monitor your child's television viewing and select age-appropriate entertainment for her. Don't let her watch anything that you know makes her afraid, even if she seems to enjoy the programme at the time. If your child is a toddler, play quietly together at bedtime or read a pleasant story. Playing soothing music may also help calm her down and clear her mind of fears.

If your child is having recurrent bad dreams, try to make her feel safe and protected before she goes to sleep. Use her playful imagination to help her get over her fears. For example:

- Go around the room on a 'monster hunt'. Look under the bed, in the wardrobe, behind the curtains and then declare the room 'officially monster-free'.
- Hang a 'No Entry to Monsters' sign on her door.
- Take an empty spray bottle, make an anti-monster label, stick it on the bottle and 'spray' the room.
- Keep a nightlight that is decorated with a favourite character close to the bed.
- Close the doors to any scary cupboards.

If your child wakes from a frightening dream, your best response is to comfort her and put her back to bed when she is calm. Stay with her until she falls asleep again. If she is old enough to talk about the dream and seems to want to tell you about it, let her. If she doesn't want to discuss it, or you suspect that there are other 'real' anxieties underlying the nightmare, choose a quiet and relaxed time during the day to ask her if she has any worries. Just giving a child the opportunity to talk things through can resolve stressful issues and stop them building up in her mind.

Night terrors

Night terrors are often confused with nightmares, but they differ in a few important ways:

1 Nightmares are bad dreams that occur during REM sleep, whereas night terrors happen during the deepest stage of non-REM sleep.

2 Nightmares often occur deep in the night, while night terrors tend to happen within the first few hours after falling asleep.

3 A child having a night terror is very difficult to rouse or comfort and may become more upset when you try, whereas a child having a nightmare can usually be woken and consoled quite easily.

By observing your child when she wakes in fear in the night you will be able to determine whether she is having a nightmare or a night terror.

When a child experiences a night terror she may wake up screaming, wide-eyed, terrified, confused, incoherent, disoriented and hallucinating. Sometimes the child may run around helplessly and mistake objects and people as dangers. Her pupils will be dilated, her heart beats fast and she will most likely be sweating. The episode might last for between 10 and 30 minutes before she falls asleep again.

Night terrors occur most often between the ages of three and eight years, and they tend to run in families. The cause of these terrors is unknown, although it is possible they are triggered by being over-tired. Although these night terrors are very frightening for parents to witness, the child is unaware of what is happening and will not remember anything about it in the morning.

Dealing with night terrors

O During night terrors parents should repeat soothing comments slowly, such as, 'You are fine. Mummy and Daddy are here.' Be patient, as a night terror can last up to 30 or 40 minutes.

O Never wake your child during a terror as it can frighten her. Don't shout at her or shake her, you can't 'snap her out of it'. Touching and holding your child may feel like the right thing to do, but if it makes the situation worse, don't do it.

O Don't be upset if your child gets angry or strikes out at you. She's reacting to the object of her terror, not you.

O Be sure to protect the child from injury. If there are repeated episodes, night-terror-proof her bedroom. Remove anything she might trip over or that might fall on her as she is thrashing around. Watch the episode from the sidelines, intervening only if she's in danger of hurting herself, then gently try to direct the child back to bed.

O Provide your toddler with a safe place to sleep. Pick up toys, lock or bar the windows and use a stair gate. Never put children who have night terrors on the top bunk.

O Warn babysitters, and any other people who may be with your child at night, about the terrors so they don't over-react if it happens.

Most children outgrow night terrors in the primary-school years, but in the meantime there a few things you can do to reduce the frequency of their occurence. Research has shown that night terrors are more likely to occur if a child is over-tired, so be even more vigilant in following a good sleep routine. You might also consider bringing bedtime forward a little or giving your child a brief nap or rest period to help ensure that she does not get over-tired.

Although she may seem too young for it, it is also possible that your child may be suffering from stress. Find out if there is anything bothering her, but don't mention the night terrors – that might worry her, especially as she probably doesn't remember them. Continual night terrors can be a sign of illness, so make sure she isn't over-tired, reacting to medicines or suffering from a food allergy. If you are concerned, seek medical advice – especially if you notice drooling, jerking or stiffening during the terror.

Parasomnias

A parasomnia can be one of a number of sleep disorders, including sleepwalking, teeth grinding, rhythmic movement disorder and restless leg syndrome. All these conditions occur during partial arousals in sleep or during transitions between wakefulness and sleep. They are more common in children than in adults and seem to run in families.

Sleepwalking

Research suggests that sleepwalking is experienced by as many as 40 per cent of children, so it is a common problem. It usually occurs between the ages of three and seven and more frequently among boys than girls. The sleepwalking habit also appears to run in families. If sleepwalking starts at an early age, it will generally disappear as the child gets older – at approximately 13 years and eight or nine months.

Sleepwalkers have different patterns – some walk only a few times a year and others might do it almost every night – but it usually occurs just an hour or two after falling asleep when children are in the stage of deep sleep.

An episode will begin with the child sitting up in bed and repeating certain movements, such as rubbing her eyes or fumbling with her clothes. She may then get out of bed and walk around, or even out of the room. As well as sleepwalking the child will often speak or mumble and can urinate. She may look dazed and her movements and speech may be clumsy; usually when you talk to her she will not answer you. The whole period of sleepwalking tends to lasts between five and 20 minutes.

What to do if your child sleepwalks

O When you find your child sleepwalking you should gently guide her back to bed. Don't yell or make a loud noise to wake her up and don't shake her; she is asleep, so treat her as you would if she was asleep in her bed.

O As sleep deprivation can often contribute to sleepwalking, make sure your child is getting enough sleep. Consult the sleep charts on pages 26–9 and, if necessary, bring forward her bedtime. Aside from that, stick to a regular bedtime routine and keep the stimulation before bedtime to a calm level.

○ A full bladder may trigger an episode, so restrict the amount of fluids she drinks before bedtime.

○ Remove anything from the bedroom that could be hazardous or harmful to a child. Keep doors and windows closed; if your child doesn't like to have the door closed when she goes to sleep, leave it ajar and fix a small bell on the door frame. When your child sleepwalks and opens the door, the ringing bell will alert you.

○ Hypnosis has been found to be helpful for both children and adults.

Sleeptalking

Most often this shows itself as talking, laughing or crying out while asleep. It is very common among children, with up to 50 per cent of children reported as speaking in their sleep. As with the other parasomnias, the child is unaware of what she is doing and will have no memory of the incident the next day. Sometimes parents can become concerned if their child is crying in her sleep, but generally there is no cause for alarm and no need to find a solution for it, as most children will grow out of it.

Teeth grinding (bruxism)

This habit features grinding or clenching of teeth during sleep. Approximately 15 to 30 per cent of children grind their teeth, and normally they start to do so when their baby teeth emerge. Most children lose the bruxism habit after they get permanent teeth.

Grinding of baby teeth rarely results in problems. However, bruxism can cause headaches, pain in the jaw and wear on the teeth. Consult your dentist if your child's teeth look worn or if your child complains of tooth sensitivity or pain.

There is a view that children grind their teeth when they are under stress, so make sure your child is in a calm and relaxed state before falling asleep. It is a good idea to include plenty of water in your child's diet, too, because dehydration may be related to teeth grinding.

Rhythmic movement disorder

Otherwise known as RMD, rhythmic movement disorder is a condition characterized by repetitive banging or rocking motions just before and during light sleep. This condition occurs primarily in infants and young children, although adults can be affected as well. Some parents worry that it is a sign of distress or even psychological disturbance, although there is no evidence that this is so.

The repetitive movements occur in certain areas of the body, usually the head and neck, and there are varying types of movement which may be seen:

○ Head-banging – the child moves her head backwards and forwards.

○ Body-rocking – the child gets onto her hands and knees and rocks her whole body backwards and forwards. Parents whose child soothes herself to sleep in this way may hear the cot moving vigorously in the night. In the morning they may find that their child's exertions have moved the cot several centimetres.

o Head-rolling – the head moves from side to side while your child is in lying on her back, face up.

o Body-rolling – the whole body moves laterally while in a supine position.

RMD most commonly affects healthy children, although it may also be seen in association with autism and other developmental disorders. There is no consensus about what causes this condition, although it often seems to be associated with self-soothing activities. For most affected children RMD is a self-limited condition that does not require treatment. However, if your child exhibits particularly violent movements, it can be helpful to secure protective padding around the sides of the cot or bed.

Medical conditions affecting sleep
Restless leg syndrome

Restless leg syndrome (RLS) is a common cause of painful legs and in children it is often described as 'growing pains'. RLS is a movement disorder that includes uncomfortable and unpleasant feelings in the legs (such as crawly, tingly or itchy) that give the child an overwhelming urge to move; although often a child with restless leg syndrome can have difficulty describing the specific sensations.

RLS is usually particularly marked during the night because the condition worsens when the child lies down. This makes it difficult for the child to fall asleep, and so she will have a disturbed and restless sleep, which may result in hyperactivity or lack of attention during the day.

This condition tends to run in families, so if there is a familial tendency to RLS, any limb pains that come on at night should be referred to a doctor. RLS can be treated with changes in bedtime routines, increased iron in the diet and possibly medications.

Snoring

Many, if not most, children snore on occasion and about 10 per cent or more habitually snore. Children who are over three tend to snore during the deeper stages of sleep.

Loud and regular nightly snoring may be abnormal in otherwise healthy children, but snoring can also be caused by nasal congestion or by enlarged adenoids or tonsils that block the airway. So sometimes snoring is a sign of a respiratory infection, a stuffy nose or allergy and will stop once the child is well again. Some children who snore, though, may have sleep apnoea.

Sleep apnoea

About 1–3 per cent of children not only snore but also suffer from breathing problems during their sleep. When snoring is accompanied by gasps or pauses in breathing, the child may have OSA: obstructive sleep apnoea.

Sleep apnoea is characterized by pauses in breathing during sleep, caused by blocked airways, and results in repeated arousal from sleep. Sleep apnoea has been associated with daytime sleepiness, academic problems and hyperactivity.

The effects of sleep apnoea last beyond the night, and during the day parents may observe some or all of the following:

○ In the morning children with sleep apnoea are chronically tired and will be difficult to rouse for school. Once up, they are lethargic and listless.

○ They may be irritable, agitated or aggressive and may find it difficult to make friends because poor-quality sleep affects their behaviour. Occasionally children with OSA are wrongly labelled with ADHD because negative or aggressive behaviour in children is often attributed to attention-deficit or behaviour disorders. The fact that it could be due to sleep deprivation is often overlooked.

○ Children with OSA will function at below their optimal level because of the tiredness they experience. They are likely to under-achieve at school and may have school-related behaviour problems as a consequence.

○ A child might complain about headaches during the day, and especially in the morning.

○ The next day the child will be sleepy and may even fall asleep or daydream because she has been constantly roused during the night and so has not had enough nourishing sleep.

○ Children with OSA often speak with a nasal quality to their voice and breathe regularly through the mouth.

Talk to your child's doctor if any of the following symptoms are observed:

○ Your child is having problems breathing or her breathing is noisy.

○ Your child snores loudly and on a regular basis.

○ Her breathing pauses during sleep or she gasps and snorts or even stops breathing.

○ She is restless or sleeps in abnormal positions with her head in an unusual position.

○ She sweats heavily while asleep.

○ She has difficulty getting up in the morning, even after the proper amount of sleep.

○ Your child experiences unusual night-time awakenings.

○ She has difficulty falling asleep and staying asleep.

○ She is very sleepy and/or starts to demonstrate behavioural problems.

Causes and treatment of sleep apnoea

○ The most common cause of OSA in childhood is the enlargement of the tonsils in the back of the throat and the adenoids in the back of the nose. Tonsils and adenoids grow most quickly when a child is between the ages of two and seven. Having the tonsils and adenoids removed has been shown to cure OSA in 80–90 per cent of children. Sometimes the adenoids grow back again, and if the symptoms return, your child may need more surgery.

○ Obesity is another cause of childhood OSA. Children who are very obese (overweight) need to start an exercise and weight-management programme.

○ Long-term allergies or hay fever may also cause OSA. These can usually be treated.

○ Children with certain medical conditions associated with weak muscles or low muscle tone, such as Down's syndrome, are more likely to have OSA.

○ If you suspect your child may have symptoms of sleep apnoea, talk to your doctor, who may refer her to a sleep specialist and/or an overnight sleep study.

○ Children with special conditions or severe sleep apnoea may need a machine to help them breathe at night. This is called continuous positive airways pressure (CPAP), which delivers air into the airways through a specially designed nasal mask or pillow.

What to do if things go wrong

Problem: Insomnia

If your child complains of difficulty falling asleep, remaining asleep and/or early morning awakenings, she is most likely suffering from insomnia.

After the initial stage of struggling to get to sleep, a child can become very distressed about her inability to sleep. This worry can cause further insomnia, which in turn can set up a chronic sleep-deprivation cycle. Short-term insomnia can arise because of stress, pain, or a medical or psychiatric condition, but it can become a long-term problem if the underlying cause is not addressed or if healthy sleep practices are not employed.

If you think your child's insomnia is the result of underlying medical or psychological conditions you should seek professional help. However, if there are no medical reasons, developing good sleep practices and maintaining a consistent sleep schedule can be enough to improve her ability to fall asleep and stay asleep.

Solution: Prepare your child for sleep

- Make sure your child has a good 'wind-down' routine before bedtime, as outlined in Chapter 3.
- Avoid exercise in the two hours before bedtime, as this stimulates rather than tires the body.
- Do not give her any drinks containing caffeine, including hot chocolate.
- Make sure her bedroom is an environment that is conducive to sleep: it should be dark, quiet and coolish.
- Remove the television and other stimulating media from the bedroom.
- Teach your child a few relaxation techniques to reduce her muscular tension.
- A high-carb snack at dinner, such as a banana, could help promote relaxation, but avoid fatty, spicy and high-protein foods shortly before bedtime.

○ If your child has an over-active mind or is worried about something in her life, try playing relaxing music or talking books to help her to take her mind off whatever is bothering her.

Problem: Fear of the dark

We have already seen in Chapter 5 that being alone in the dark can give rise to fears and fantasies. Many children experience night-time fears at some point in their young life, but in imaginative and sensitive children these dreams can make them 'hysterical with fear' – as this mother describes in an email to raisingkids.co.uk:

Our five-year-old daughter is an only child. She's been a diffi-cult sleeper since birth but has now developed a severe fear of the dark. Every night she wakes crying, saying she's had a bad dream, and comes into our bedroom. It takes her ages to go back to sleep in her own room. We have left numerous night-lights on in the hall and her room but she becomes hysterical with fear if we ignore her. My husband and I are now so fed up with it that we are resorting to shouting at her and smacking her, which is distressing for all of us. She's very well-behaved in the day and very mature for her age, although she won't go upstairs by herself during the day. She's also a very clingy girl and it has taken us a year to be able finally to drop her off at school without her crying! Is this all related?

This poor child's fear of the dark is so great that she is prepared to be punished rather than be alone. When she wakes in the night her mind is flooded with fears and anxieties and she becomes very afraid and unable to go back to sleep. So, scared and alone, she seeks reassurance and comfort with her parents.

As her parents, sleep is also broken they react, like many other people who suffer from chronic sleep deprivation, in an unconsidered way. 'Shouting and smacking' doesn't work, so something else is required. This child is not coming to her parents' room because she wants company, or a drink of water, or just a kiss and a cuddle; she is, by their own admission, 'hysterical with fear'. In this situation, her fears are genuine and sending her back to bed isn't the solution.

Solution: Managing her fear

o This type of problem usually occurs among sensitive and imaginative children, and dealing with it does take time. There is no instant solution to the problem which will allow everyone a full night's sleep in their own bed, undisturbed. However, if she can start off in her own bed with lots of lights on, it does show that she can sleep in her own bed.

o In such a case of extreme fear, when no one is getting a decent night's sleep, a parent should give up trying to get their child to stay in her own bed, alone. Instead, put a mattress on the floor next to your bed so that if she wakes she can come into your room and sleep there, thus stopping the cycle in the short term. In the longer term you could encourage her to stay in her room by using the technique of moving the mattress nearer to the bedroom door, as described on page 144.

o Knowing she can go to your room without reproach may be just enough to take the edge off her fear. Alternatively, you could let her come into your bed until her fear subsides and then, when she has calmed down, take her back to her own room.

o The fear a child experiences at night can become connected to her bedroom itself and sometimes to the extent that the child won't even go there alone during daylight. Try to remove some of this fear by spending time with her in her bedroom doing pleasurable things, such as reading, playing or just sitting together and chatting. Take your time with this until she is able to spend time there alone. All of this will help her be able to stay in her bed when she wakes at night.

Differences in temperament play an important part in so many matters to do with children. In this example the mother wonders if her daughter's behaviour at night is related to the fact that her daughter took a long time to settle at school and is often 'clingy'. It is very much related: this is her child's temperament. Children differ in how much independence from their parents they need and this little girl clearly likes to be close to people she is attached to, is more dependent on them and takes time to adjust to new situations. So when she wakes up scared in the night, it is these people and their comfort that she needs.

This is not a unique example by any means: starting school and other changes in the family can unsettle most children, but they can also cause vulnerable children to become nervous and anxious. Even adults feel alone in the small hours of the morning, but a child can become fearful of many things. As children settle into school, deal with other changes and grow in confidence, the problem often fades away.

Such a situation requires the parents to be patient. It will take time to resolve because they are dealing with something that stems from their child's personality. The solution outlined above is not ideal in the short term, but it is better than having her 'hysterical with fear'.

Problem: Intrusive night 'visions' before falling asleep

Many children of all ages become anxious just before they fall asleep. This is because, as they relax into sleep, the worries that were suppressed during the day surge into their mind, forcing them into a fearful wakefulness. Scared and upset, they are then unable to fall asleep. In this example, a 10-year-old had particularly upsetting thoughts as she drifted off to sleep:

My 10-year-old is having 'visions' of a graveyard, a headstone with her own name on it and the rest of the family standing around it, crying. This happens only at bedtimes when she closes her eyes, although it's not quite a dream. Otherwise she is a happy, healthy child. I have checked with her teachers who have told me that there is nothing unusual about her behaviour during the day and her school work is as good as ever. I have tried talking to my daughter and sleeping in the same bed as her, but I just don't know what to try next. How do I get to the bottom of the problem? Please help – this has been going on for a couple of months now.

This would be an alarming situation for any parent – but it is simply that a sensitive girl is expressing fears she has in her subconscious. Very imaginative children (of which she seems to be one) experience their fears as what this mother refers to as a 'vision'. Dreams occur during REM sleep, not as a person drifts off, so it is not a dream, but more likely thoughts she has put to the back of her mind during the day, which now come to the forefront when she is alone and with no other distractions.

Solution: Talk it through

o In this example the girl is worried about dying, which is not an uncommon fear to have around the age of 10. She may also be frightened by something she has seen on television, read in the newspaper or heard in the playground. These are very general worries that are common to children of this age, which she has 'personalized' in her vision of the graveyard.

● Alternatively, there could be something at home or school that is causing her distress. Is she being bullied? Is she worried about moving to a new secondary school? Even primary school can be very stressful these days, with SATS and the like to contend with. Moreover, this is the age at which children enter adolescence, which can be a very difficult time for them.

● Find a time during the day when she is relaxed and happy and talk to her about what she sees when she closes her eyes. Explain to her that her fears and her 'vision' may be simply the way her subconscious expresses worries that she keeps hidden during the day. Ask her if she's worried about dying. Is she scared of being ill or does she know anyone who is ill? Does she have some symptoms that she believes are indicative of a serious illness? Are there changes to her body that she is concerned about? Could she have had some menstrual bleeding and has not mentioned it to you? By discussing the meaning of the 'vision' you will bring her real fears out into the open and then she will be able to resolve them during the day in her conscious mind.

● She has probably begun to associate the 'vision' with bedtime, so now her fear and anticipation of going to sleep cause it to occur. One way of dealing with this problem is to break the cycle and help her to develop new and relaxing associations with bedtime. Try reading with her to help her sleep, get her to take a relaxing bath or put on the radio or a talking story to distract her.

Teach your child to relax

Progressive relaxation is a technique that involves relaxing the body's muscle groups in a progressive sequence: moving upwards from the feet towards the head. Starting at the toes, tense them, then relax them. Move to the feet and ankles, repeat the tense, then relax. Slowly move up the body towards the head in this way – tensing and then relaxing each part.

Diaphragmatic breathing is another technique that aids relaxation by breathing air deep into the lungs as a result of inhaling from the diaphragm rather than breathing shallowly. As the air enters through the nose, count to four and allow your stomach to expand. Then breathe out through the mouth for a count of four. Repeat this several times. By concentrating on taking deep breaths, holding your breath to a count of three and then exhaling slowly, you will help your body become more relaxed.

O Help your child to develop some relaxation strategies, so that by the time she goes to bed she isn't tense and anxious (see the above box).

Don't forget

O Night waking through fear can stem from something your child has read or seen, so monitor her television viewing and select age-appropriate entertainment for her. Don't let her watch anything that you know makes her afraid and try to talk to her during the day to see if anything is troubling her.

O If your child is fearful at night, use the bedtime routine to make her feel safe and protected before she goes to sleep; play quietly or read a pleasant story together, and de-monster the bedroom if need be!

O Sleep deprivation can contribute to sleepwalking, so make sure she is getting enough sleep.

O Observe your child during the day as well as at night to determine why she is waking at night, and whether it is because of illness, stress, anxiety or perhaps something which you might need to talk to your child's doctor about, such as sleep apnoea.

O Most children will experience night-time fears in their young lives; if you think they are genuinely afraid, don't punish them, but give them the comfort that they need to be able to return to sleep.

Early risers

This is a book about sleep issues, but often a child who wakes up bright and very early can be just as real a problem for parents as waking in the night or resisting sleep. It may sound poetic to say that your child is a 'lark' when you're an 'owl', but in practice early waking can leave adults drained of energy.

It's often supposed that children are born either larks or owls, but in fact just 10 to 15 per cent of children have a strong genetic predisposition towards one or the other. A study by Stanford University in 1998 identified a gene mutation – a so-called 'clock gene' – that seemed to be an indicator of whether someone had a predisposition to wake up much earlier or later than normal. If you are the 'owl' parents of a 'lark' child, who is chirpy and ready to go in the early hours of the morning when you are in need of another hour or two of sleep, whether this habit is learned or innate will be of little interest to you if it doesn't offer a solution to the problem!

The good news is that, because circadian rhythms are tuned to a 25-hour day, a more common occurrence is for children to become more like owls than larks. It is the impo-sition of regular routines for sleeping and eating that keeps most children running on a 24-hour schedule. However, this schedule has to work with the child's nature as an owl or lark, too, and in some cases it can prove impossible to encourage a lark to completely match the owl habits of their family.

Early rising – whose problem is it?

A common reason for early waking is simply that your child has had enough sleep. If your child is waking after a full night's replenishing sleep, he doesn't have a sleep problem. If you're unsure whether or not he is getting enough sleep, take a good look at the charts on pages 26–9 and add up your child's night and day sleep. A two-year-old should be sleeping 13 hours a day on average, broken down into two hours of naps and the remainder as night sleep. If your two-year-old naps for two hours in the afternoon and goes to bed at 7 p.m., it's no surprise that he is waking up full of beans at 6 a.m. After all, he has had a good night's sleep and is now ready to face the day.

You can't expect your child to sleep longer in the morning simply because the family doesn't stir until an hour or two later, but it can be a real problem if the household usually gets going at 7 a.m. and your child is fully awake and calling for attention from 5 a.m. In this case there are two alternatives: you can gradually shift his bedtime until he is going to bed later and waking up later in the morning – although delaying bedtime is not always guaranteed to work – or you can try the less appealing alternative which is that you go to bed earlier so that *you* are also wide awake at 5 a.m. and better able to get up with your child. Whatever the solution, the aim is to get your child's sleeping habits to coincide with those of the rest of the family.

Is your child getting enough sleep at night?

Below are some of the questions you should ask yourself to determine whether or not your child is getting enough night sleep:

- Is he drowsy and lethargic first thing in the morning? Or is he happy and alert when he wakes up?
- Does he have a morning nap within an hour or so of waking up?
- If you take him into your bed in the early morning, does he fall asleep quickly and sleep for over an hour?
- Is he an unenthusiastic eater first thing in the morning?
- What is his overall energy level in the morning? Is he most energetic sometime between the late morning and early afternoon?

So, check with the sleep charts to see if your child is getting enough sleep, but remember that they give an average figure and that 10–15 per cent of children will fall on either side of it. Work back from his waking-up time and calculate the number of hours of sleep your child is getting at night. Look at his naps, too, if he has them, and include these in the total. If your child's early-rising problem has been going on for some time, it's a good idea to start a sleep diary.

Keeping a sleep diary

Every day for a week, write down your child's bedtime and waking times – don't try to remember them but write them down each time. Don't forget to include any naps and other periods of sleep, such as when he drops off in the car or in the pushchair.

○ *Going-to-bed-time/going-to-sleep-time.* These times may not be the same, as your child may be lying awake in his cot or bed for some time before he actually falls asleep. How long it takes your child to drop off will tell you if your child is really tired when he is put to bed. As a rule of thumb, if a child falls asleep within 15 minutes of being put into his cot or bed, his bedtime is correct.

○ *Waking-up time.* Note the time that he gets up and assess your child's demeanour. Did he wake spontaneously or did you rouse him inadvertently by going into his room? Is your child content to play alone in his cot or bed after waking up? Does your child fall asleep again if he is left alone? On waking is he lively and alert or still drowsy and half asleep?

○ If your child is still having daytime naps, enter the start and finish time of both his morning and afternoon naps.

○ Total all the sleep sessions over the week and again compare with the average, bearing in mind that your child may be one of the 10 per cent or so who need more or less sleep than the average.

When you have kept a sleep diary for a week, certain differences from the norm may become clear. Look at your observations and consider how your child's sleep time is distributed. Is he having more daytime sleep than average and less night-time sleep? How does his waking-up time relate to his going-to-sleep time? Remember that it is not 'abnormal' for a two-year-old to wake up at 5 a.m. if you take into account the fact that he is going to sleep, for instance, eleven hours earlier at 6 p.m. Is he sleeping regularly in the car or pushchair?

Why is he waking up?

It's always worth investigating whether outside factors are at work in waking up your child, if he would naturally sleep for longer when left undisturbed. When you next go into your child's bedroom in the morning, take a moment to look at his sleep environment.

Is the room too bright?

If your child's room is east-facing or has a large window, he may be waking up as his room gets brighter – this is particularly true in the summer months. If you haven't already installed them, try putting up black-out blinds or thicker curtains in an effort to block out light and induce him to sleep later. If he is in an east-facing room, the sun will be shining directly into his room as it rises, so check the position of his bed. If his bed is right in the line of the morning sun, move it to a shadier part of the room.

Is a noise waking him up?

It could be that your child isn't waking up naturally but is being disturbed by a particular noise that can be heard at a regular time each morning. Perhaps the central heating rattles when it goes on in the morning. Does his room over-look a road with heavy morning traffic? It may be that a neighbour gets up early and he can hear her alarm clock or her moving around and he is responding to that. If noise is the culprit, you might consider – if possible – moving him to a different bedroom. If that's not feasible, setting the radio to a talk-show channel at a low volume will produce a 'white noise' effect that may block out other external sounds.

Is he too warm/too cold?

If your child is prone to throwing off his bedcovers and wak-ing up because he's too cold, it may be worth investing in clips that secure his blanket or duvet in place. For small babies a specially designed baby sleeping bag will make sure he is kept warm, however restless he is. Alternatively, it may be that your child is too warm, in which case you

Old habits die hard...

If your child has got into the habit of waking up early, whatever the reason, it means he's had time to settle into a pattern which you'll have to break if you want to reclaim the early morning for yourself. As with all habits, you'll probably meet resistance at first when you try to change it. But you can succeed, given time. Keep that in mind and stay firm and help your child to reset his body clock.

should look at the setting on any radiators in his room or consider leaving his window open a little at night.

He's hungry

If your child is waking too early and is either tucking into a bottle with vigour or complaining about hunger pains, you should be wary of establishing a habit of a 4–5 a.m. feed. Make sure a toddler has a good supper, with an additional healthy snack if he wants it, which should allow a slow release of sugar and help him sleep through the night.

If your child already wakes up early in the morning demanding food, this is a habit that you can wean him off. Resist running into his room at his first cry and delay offering him food until a while after he wakes. Eventually he will learn that waking early does not result in getting food and he will either settle himself back to sleep or won't wake up in the first place.

Toilet time

If your child is calling out because his nappy is full or he wants to go to the toilet, there are a few solutions:

o Avoid giving him a large drink just before he goes to bed, but do make it available to him if he needs it.

o Once an older child is toilet-trained, you can teach him that he can go to the toilet without being accompanied by you. Leave the hallway and bathroom lights on when you go to bed at night so that any trips to the loo are made safely and happily.

Quiz – Is your child a lark or an owl?

If your child could choose his bedtime, what time would he go to bed?

Before seven = 0

After seven = 1

If he could choose what time he woke up, would it be:

Before 6 a.m. = 0

After 6 a.m. = 1

At what time of day does he have the most energy?

Morning = 0

Early afternoon = 1

Late afternoon/early evening = 2

Night = 3

If the score is 2 or under, he's a lark. If the score is 4 or above, he's an owl.

Toddlers

Life is very exciting for toddlers. For some children, when they wake in the early hours of the morning, there are so many fascinating things they can do that they want to get up there and then and do them. If only they understood that night-time is for sleeping and not for playing, especially when they come into their parents' bedroom looking for someone to play with. So how can you get across to a two-year-old that night-time means sleep time?

Using light and dark

By the age of two your child will know that darkness means it's bedtime and that daylight usually means it's time to get up. You can reinforce this message by making the room bright and light when it's time to get up and dark, cosy and womb-like when it's bedtime.

Once your child has grasped this concept of day and night you can use it to your advantage. If your child wakes up at, say, 5 a.m., you should respond to him as if it's the middle of the night. Don't engage him in conversation, make it clear that he's made a mistake and it's night-time and encourage him to return to sleep as you would in the middle of the night. If you don't want him (or you) to get up at 5 a.m. every day, it's up to you to respond clearly and firmly in setting this boundary.

To reinforce the message that night-time is for sleeping, some parents make a big production of saying 'good night to everything' before they put their child to bed by going around the house with him and saying goodnight to everything that he associates with daytime activity. This includes his toys, the kitchen, the fridge, the television, the furniture and so on. Then they explain that at night-time everything is quiet and asleep and everything wakes up only when it is light, concluding with the message that he should also go to sleep now that it's dark and get up only when it becomes light.

Consistency

If you want to ensure that your child sleeps well and wakes at the right time, approach any sleep training with consistency. There's no point in establishing a routine during the week and then relaxing it at the weekends, as this will only confuse your child and you may have to start from scratch every Monday!

The clock says no!

Some parents find the use of toddler clocks helps younger children understand when they've woken up too early. From around the age of three, your child can be reasoned with and you can explain to him the notion of waking up too early. Toddler clocks – which use pictures rather than numbers to tell children the time – can be set to what you think is an acceptable time for waking up and at that hour the clock will signal to the child that it is time to get up. For instance, some clocks feature a bunny whose eyes are closed when it's sleeping time, so you can explain to your child that when the bunny is sleeping he should be too and that he can leave his room to wake others only when the bunny is awake.

Early morning entertainment

If your child has reached the age of three or above and is still an early waker, this habit may have become deeply ingrained or he may simply be a natural lark. The longer a habit has had to develop and become entrenched, the harder it is to retrain your child. A more workable solution in this case may be to look at what your child can do to entertain himself when he wakes so that he doesn't feel the need to wake up others to entertain him.

With younger children, while you won't want them wandering around the house by themselves, you can teach them how to amuse themselves in their bedroom without disturbing you. One idea is to create a 'morning basket' which is filled with toys that they can play with if they wake up in the morning. Change what is in there regularly so there is always something new and interesting. Don't forget to keep anything that makes a noise or plays a tune out of the basket unless you want to be awakened by it too!

This is also a good age at which to teach your child not to disturb you too early. You can agree a number of signals

Playtime without playmates

Teaching children to entertain themselves is a valuable life lesson. Not only will it allow you time to sleep or get on with other things, it also helps them to become independent of you and develop their inner resources.

When the clocks change

Be aware of when the clocks are changing for summer and winter and plan ahead as to how you're going to respond six days before it happens. Set your clock either forward or back 10 minutes a day until after six days you've reached the new time – that way you're not expecting your child to go to sleep an hour earlier than usual, or wake up an hour later than he is accustomed to.

with him (in addition to the toddler clock), such as hearing your alarm clock go off, which mean that it's okay to come into your room. You could also agree that when you're ready to be woken up by your children, you'll leave your bedroom door ajar.

If all else fails… there's a reason why children's television channels such as CBeebies begin so early in the morning! Older children (from five and above) can be given a greater margin of movement – you can let them turn on the television, for example, as long as the sound isn't too loud, or they can amuse themselves with music or a story-book CD as they can usually work stereos by themselves too. Keep an eye on them, though, and make sure that they are not forcing themselves awake just so they can get up to go and watch one of their favourite programmes.

What to do when things go wrong

Problem: Early waking despite a late bedtime

My 12-month-old son regularly wakes up at 5 a.m. – sometimes a little either side. I have tried moving his bedtime later but to no avail. How late he goes to bed doesn't seem to make any difference to the morning. What can I do?

Solution: Earlier to bed

● According to Dr Marc Weissbluth, paediatrician and leading expert on children's sleep disorders, the *leading cause* of early waking in children over the age of four months is having too late a bedtime.

● It may sound counter-intuitive, but often bringing forward the time you put your child to bed can help him to sleep later and re-establish his sleep–wake rhythms. This is because sometimes children get over-tired and become anxious, irritable and upset – all of which make it harder for them to fall asleep and to enjoy quality sleep. By putting him to bed earlier, you may find that your child wakes up later.

● Again, check the amount of night sleep your child is getting and compare it to the average for his age. If your child's bedtime is too late compared to the average, gradually move his bedtime forward by 15 minutes for three or four days; go through your usual bedtime rituals, but start the process 15 minutes earlier.

● If your child settles at this earlier time – *even if he doesn't wake any later in the morning* – move it forward again by another 15 minutes on the following three or four evenings.

○ Continue to move bedtime forward until your child no longer falls asleep within 15 minutes. At this point, move bedtime back to the point at which he was regularly falling asleep within 15 minutes of being put in his cot.

○ It may take some time for the waking hour to become later. During the whole process of moving bedtime forward, don't go to him when he wakes in the early hours; give him time and he may settle back to sleep. Don't go in to change his nappy or give him a bottle.

Problem: Regular bedtime routine, but still up with the lark

My daughter, who is nine months old, wakes every morning at 5.30 a.m. or so and no matter what we do she wants to be up and about. She has a regular evening routine and settles down easily at around 6 p.m. How can I get her to sleep later in the morning?

An average child of nine months needs 11.5 hours at night. If a child is going to sleep at 6 p.m., his waking time would be between 5 a.m. and 6 a.m. This little girl is waking at 5.30 a.m. because she went to bed at 6 p.m.! If this is too early for the family, the solution is to move the whole sleep cycle to coincide with the family's habits.

Unlike a child who is being kept up in the evening past his 'natural' bedtime, the child in this example *is* sleeping enough. A child who is waking early after a full night's sleep will probably need a nap early in the day and perhaps again in the afternoon and will be ready for bed by the early evening. The whole sleep–wake cycle has shifted.

There is a predictable sleep–wake cycle but it is running one or two hours ahead of the rest of the family's. This is sometimes referred to as an early sleep phase; it is less common than a late sleep phase and is generally seen only in infants. In such a situation the aim is to shift the child's sleeping pattern so that everything happens later than it currently does. This can and should be done slowly, so that the child doesn't resist the changes.

Solution: Shift the whole sleep–wake cycle

o Simply keeping a child up later in the evening will not usu-ally be enough to solve this problem. Keeping him awake beyond his normal bedtime may make him fretful and ir-ritable, so he will find it difficult to drop off when placed in bed. What needs to be changed is not just his time for bed but his whole sleep–wake cycle, including naps. Mealtimes will also need to be shifted as part of this process.

o Start by keeping your child up 10 minutes later for his morning nap. Make the afternoon nap 10 minutes later and then put your child to bed 10 minutes later than usual. By doing this you are altering his sleep phase – hopefully with the result that your child wakes up 10 minutes later. Keep pushing all the sleep times back in this way, little by little, until your child is waking at a more sociable hour.

What time for bedtime?

Finding the right bedtime for your child can often involve an amount of to-ing and fro-ing. Make small changes and wait and see what happens, remembering that the longer a habit has been established, the more difficult it will be to change.

○ It is easier to control times of going to bed and sleep than it is waking times. The child is therefore likely to resist change here and for the first week or two there may be no change to his waking time. It can often take a couple of weeks to produce a significant change in the sleep cycle, so do persevere.

Problem: Up at dawn and ready for the day

For the last week or so my son has been waking at 4 in the morning, full of energy and wanting to play. No matter what we do – including bringing him into our bed – he won't go back to sleep. He usually falls asleep between 6.30 p.m. and 9 p.m. in the evening and has one or two naps per day.

Many children have sleep problems because they don't have a regular sleep routine. This lack of sleep routine can affect other aspects of the child's life such as mealtimes, which are fitted in around naps and so the knock-on effect is that mealtimes also become irregular and erratic.

If a child goes to bed early one night and very late the next, sometimes naps once in the day and sometimes twice, the circadian rhythms can become badly disrupted. In time this lack of structure will begin to disrupt the sleep–wake cycle.

Children's bodily rhythms become regularized into a 24-hour sleep–wake pattern if they are set and maintained by certain events that always occur at the same time. The most important of these are waking in the morning, going to bed at night, napping, mealtimes and exposure to dark and light. Without this structure your child's body does not know if it should be awake or asleep.

Without a distinct routine, sleep patterns can become fragmented and the long night's sleep that develops when children have predictable routines does not occur. When circadian rhythms are disrupted, a child may wake at 4 a.m. and behave as if he were waking from a nap at 4 p.m. – he will be bright, alert and ready to play!

Solution: Reinforce natural sleep–wake rhythms

o In order to combat early waking, it is critically important to set up routines that will reprogramme the circadian rhythms. That means establishing regular getting-up times, going-to-bed times, napping and eating times.

o Consult the charts on pages 26–9 to see what the right amount of sleep is for your child. Using that information, decide on an appropriate bedtime for him by calculating the number of hours' sleep he needs and subtracting it from a desirable morning waking-up time. Work out a pleasurable and relaxing going-to-bed routine which ends with the child in his own room, in his own bed and ready to fall asleep alone (see Chapter 3). If he has been used to falling asleep elsewhere, this may be the first hurdle. (Consult Chapter 4 on how to settle your child for the night if he is resistant to going to bed.)

○ If the child has been used to a variety of different bed-times, he may not be tired at his new fixed bedtime. Tired or not, he should stay in his bed and, if necessary, initially a parent should stay with him (though not interacting with him) until he falls asleep.

○ If he has a very irregular sleep pattern, he may wake in the night. Follow the guidelines in Chapter 5 to encourage him to stay in his bed and fall asleep again.

○ Naps should be at a fixed time whether he seems tired or not. If he resists going into his cot to sleep, follow the guidelines for dealing with night-waking.

○ If he falls asleep at a time other than the designated times, wake him after 10–15 minutes.

○ Resetting a child's sleep–wake rhythms will require a considerable investment of time on the parents' part until their child is able to settle into a routine. Usually within two or three weeks, though, there will be a significant change to a more predictable sleep–wake pattern.

No pain, no gain

The longer a sleep pattern – or lack of it – has been in existence, the more difficult it will be to change, but the benefits for all once it has been established are well worth the effort.

Problem: Regular daily routine – starting at 5

My 14-month-old has a very good routine except that she wakes every morning at 5 a.m. She has two naps in the day and goes to bed at night at 7.30 p.m. without fussing and sleeps through, undisturbed, until 5 a.m. Once I wake up I can't get back to sleep. Please help!

This cry from the heart is about a child who appears to have a regular and mostly satisfactory sleep routine. The only problem is that she is waking up at least two hours before her parents would like her to. She is sleeping for 9.5 hours in total when most children of her age are sleeping for 11.5 hours. She may be one of those children who needs fewer hours than the average, but more probably she is making up for lack of night sleep elsewhere in the day.

At 14 months old this little girl is still taking two naps. In the first half of their second year most infants give up the morning nap and by 18 months old most children are napping only in the afternoon. If she is waking at 5 a.m. and sleeping again before 9 a.m., it is likely that the early morning nap is simply a continuation of night-time sleep, but a habit of waking early has developed.

Solution: Move the morning nap later

○ When a child wakes very early, having had less than the average amount of sleep, and then takes a very early morning nap (before 9 a.m.), the nap could be seen as be part of the night-time sleep which has been broken by the habit of early waking. Consult the sleep charts on pages 26–9 to identify the average sleep requirements for his age to determine whether this is the case.

○ Look at your child's daytime sleep routine. Babies and toddlers who are still taking daytime naps offer parents an opportunity to juggle daytime sleep patterns in order to influence their night sleep patterns. If your child is taking a morning nap before 9 a.m. and is tired early in the morning, this nap can also be viewed as part of the long night sleep. Your aim is to join it back to the night sleep.

○ To combine the two sleeps, keep your child awake in the morning beyond the usual time of his first nap. If he normally naps at 9 a.m., move this back to 10–10.30 a.m. You may find that as he sleeps longer in the morning this early morning nap is taken later or can be dispensed with altogether. In the latter case you will probably have to move the afternoon nap forward by a couple of hours.

○ In addition, when he wakes at 5 a.m., don't respond to his calls immediately. Let him be for 15 minutes or longer if he is not crying.

○ At first he will continue with the early waking, but as nap times get later, he should sleep later into the morning.

Accept the inevitable

It may be that, whatever you do, your 'lark' will always be awake at dawn and ready and raring to go. As he gets older he can learn to entertain himself, but while he is an infant there will come a point when you simply have to get up with him. If you are more of an owl, this will be difficult, but the last resort is about embracing the inevitable and learning to enjoy early mornings. This poem by Rumi says it all:

The breeze at dawn has secrets to tell you.
Don't go back to sleep.
You must ask for what you really want.
Don't go back to sleep.
People are going back and forth across the doorsill
Where the two worlds touch
The door is round and open.
Don't go back to sleep.

Early mornings can be a time to enjoy the peace and quiet of the day, but you can also make them a special quiet time with your child, before the business of the day begins.

And finally… it's a universal truth that the moment you persuade your child to sleep late will coincide with the moment that you have to make sure he's up on time for school!

Don't forget

O   If your child is waking up early after a full night's replenishing sleep, he doesn't have a sleep problem.

O   Keeping a sleep diary of bedtimes, waking times and naps for a week might help you see if there are any differences from the norm that might be contributing to his early waking.

O   Whatever the solution to your child's early waking, the aim is to get your child's sleeping habits to coincide with those of the rest of the family.

O   See if there are any environmental factors that are waking your child, such as light, temperature, noise or even hunger, and address them accordingly.

O   Leave toys or books within reach of your child's bed so that if he does wake early, he can amuse himself in his bedroom and not come and disturb you.

O   It may just be that your child doesn't need as much sleep as others and you might have to resign yourself to getting up earlier than you would like until he chooses to sleep later. If that is the case, try to learn to love early mornings!

10 steps to better sleep

I hope that having read this book you will have found the answer to your child's sleep problem and you will be on track to a more harmonious and restful family life.

If you're still unsure, though, in this chapter I am going to synopsize 10 key factors that you should consider in order to improve your child's sleeping habits.

1 Children need quality sleep for their mental and physical growth.

2 The sleep–wake cycle. A child's body clock and developing circadian rhythms are shaped by her parents introducing 'time cues' which are synchronized with household activities.

3 Individual differences. Children have different temperaments, and some take to sleeping routines more easily than others. Use your own judgement about what works for your child rather than rigidly imposing a routine that doesn't work for her.

4 A tired child is likely to be more active, rather than less.

5 Develop a predictable bedtime routine. A routine in the run-up to bed is the lynch pin of good sleeping habits. Once a routine is established, be consistent and stick to it.

6 Be flexible and take into account any changes in circumstances that might affect bedtime. Once the disruption is over, return to the schedule as soon as possible.

7 The longer a habit is established, the more difficult it is to change. When sleeping problems arise, deal with them promptly. Expect that it will take at least two weeks to change sleeping habits that are not deeply ingrained.

8   There are several strategies you can adopt to deal with sleep problems, although many of them are difficult to institute. Determine before you start any course of action that you have the will to go through with it.

9   Shifting waking-up times, naps and bedtimes will solve many problems.

10 Establish a sleep-friendly environment for your child: make her bedroom a place that is conducive to sleep.

Children need quality sleep for their mental and physical development

Sleep is not just a period of inactivity between periods of wakefulness; it is an important process in its own right. Sleep is as important to the growing child as eating and playing. A good sleep is as important as a good meal.

Interesting facts about sleep

- By the age of two, most children have spent more time asleep than awake. Overall, a child will spend 40 per cent of her childhood asleep.

- A new baby typically causes 400–750 hours of lost sleep for her parents in the first year.

- It is more difficult to wake a child than an adult from deep sleep. If children do wake during this sleep stage, they will often be disorientated and have no recollection of it later.

○ Night-time sleep is made up of two types of sleep: rapid eye movement (REM) or active sleep; and non-rapid eye movement (NREM) sleep, or deep sleep.

○ During the deep states of NREM sleep, blood supply to the muscles is increased, energy is restored, tissue growth and repair occur and important hormones are released for growth and development.

○ Scientists are not absolutely sure why we have REM sleep, but there are several theories, including that it is important for the consolidation of memories and learning. Others speculate that REM sleep is particularly important to the developing brain, possibly because it provides the neural stimulation that newborns need to form mature neural connections and to develop a proper nervous system.

○ Adults spend between 20–25 per cent of their sleeping time in REM sleep, while babies spend 50 per cent. Premature babies have even more REM sleep, at around 80–90 per cent, confirming the view that REM sleep has a role to play in brain development. By six months a baby's REM sleep accounts for 30 per cent of her sleep, and this declines to adult levels at around the age of three.

Don't wake up, sleepyhead!

Research confirms that sleep is vitally important for a child's physical and mental development. The younger the child, the more important sleep is to her brain development.

So why is sleep important for children?

○ Growth hormones are released during sleep and sleep is vital to proper physical and mental development.

○ Sleep aids memory and learning. In babies, REM sleep is thought to play an important role in brain development. In older children, lack of sleep has an impact on decision-making, creativity, memory and performance in school.

○ Mood and social behaviour are affected by sleep. The parts of the brain that control emotions, decision-making and social interactions slow down dramatically during sleep, allowing optimal performance when awake. Children who are sleep-deprived are often irritable and hyperactive and have more trouble controlling their emotions.

○ Sometimes sleep-deprived children show some of the symptoms of attention deficit hyperactivity disorder (ADHD), such as inattention, hyperactivity and impulsiveness. This happens because these weary children need to create a stimulating environment in order to keep themselves awake, which they need to do to be able to learn.

○ Without adequate sleep the immune system becomes weak and the body becomes more vulnerable to infection and disease.

○ Some sleep experts suggest that neurons used during the day repair themselves during sleep. When we are deprived of sleep, the nervous system is impaired.

○ New research shows that children who sleep less are more likely to be overweight.

○ Sleep problems can also affect the entire family. Tired parents will often become irritable and short-tempered.

The sleep-wake cycle

○ Circadian rhythms are regular changes in mental and physical characteristics that occur in the course of a day. These rhythms are responsive to light and dark and govern the sleep–wake cycle.

○ Left unchecked, the body runs on a 25-hour clock. The routines introduced by regular sleep and waking times maintain the 24-hour-day cycle. It is the use of 'time cues' that keep our body running with the 24-hour cycle.

○ A baby is born with its own internal clock. Initially babies are not responsive to dark–light sleep–wake cycles and will often be awake in the night and asleep in the day. Over time a baby's circadian rhythms change to resemble those of an adult.

○ By six weeks babies begin to respond to dark–light and sleep more in the night than during the day. By six months babies have long periods of night-time sleep. From six months, and often before, a baby's sleep behaviour starts to fit into that of the household.

○ According to sleep researchers, the morning wake-up time – not the bedtime – is the most important time for resetting the body clock every day.

Individual differences

○ There are general guidelines that apply to the majority of children, but not all conform to the average: 10–15 per cent of children have sleep patterns that diverge significantly from the average.

○ Babies differ by temperament. Some babies settle very easily and cry for only a little while; others are more difficult to soothe and are harder to get into a routine. This is perfectly normal. Use your intuition and your own knowledge of your baby to decide which actions to follow. Often the baby who is most difficult to settle into a routine is the one who benefits most from this structure.

○ Although based on circadian rhythms, exactly how long a child sleeps and how her sleep is scheduled are learned by 'time cues' for recurrent events throughout the day, such as waking-up time and mealtimes. Children differ in the ease with which their sleeping habits can be brought into line with household routines.

○ From eight months to eighteen months, children experience separation anxiety to varying degrees. An infant who had previously fallen asleep in her own cot without any problem may now cry pitifully as her mother leaves the room. More robust infants will be unaffected by this change.

○ Some children are stronger-willed than others and it will be more difficult to limit their behaviour when they resist settling to sleep or when they wake up in the night. Stick to your guns and hold the line. If you give in after your child

protests for 20 minutes you might as well have given in after five minutes. All you have done now is to encourage her to cry or shout for longer. What she learns is that if she goes on for long enough, she will eventually get what she wants. Remember, a good night's sleep is worth struggling for – both for you and for your child.

○ Ten–15 per cent of individuals are either larks or owls, with a distinct preference for late nights (owls) or early mornings (larks). Scientists have discovered that this pattern appears to be innate and very resistant to change.

A tired child is likely to be more active, not less

When adults get tired they slow down and are noticeably less energetic, but children do not always do so. Many children pass through the stage of being drowsy and sleepy and become over-excited and hyperactive. In this state they are more difficult to calm and get into bed. Once they are in bed, they find it more difficult to fall asleep.

Don't wait up

Parents often make the mistake of thinking that keeping a child up later will make her sleepier and ready for bed. This is not true. Children have a harder time falling asleep when they are 'over-tired'.

Is your child getting enough sleep?

Studies of primary-school children in the US revealed that nearly 40 per cent of them had some type of sleep problem, 15 per cent exhibited bedtime resistance and 10 per cent had daytime sleepiness.

Children rarely complain of sleep problems, so parents may be unaware of how much proper sleep they are actually getting. Some sleep experts theorize that sleep-deprived children seek greater stimulation during the day because they spend less time asleep at night, so their brain is active for less time then. A child will often demonstrate this by indulging in both unco-operative and attention-seeking behaviour.

Signs of sleep deprivation

The following behaviour is typical of a child who is chronically sleep-deprived:

o When travelling in the car, she almost always falls asleep.

o Every morning she has to be roused – often with difficulty.

o She seems over-tired, cranky, irritable, aggressive, over-emotional and hyperactive.

o She sometimes has difficulty thinking during the day.

o On some nights she will 'crash' much earlier than her usual bedtime.

o Her teacher might tell you that she appears sleepy (or falls asleep) at school.

Your child is getting enough sleep if she:

O Fall asleep within 15 to 30 minutes of being put to bed.

O Wakes up easily at the time she needs to get up.

O Wakes without being roused.

O Is awake and alert all day.

Develop a predictable bedtime routine

The first year is the optimal time for developing regular daytime and bedtime schedules. The key elements are consistency and predictability. When you start a routine your baby will begin to expect the next stages, often waving her arms in delight as she hears the bath filling up. This is key: the routine should be pleasurable and should also help the child look forward to falling asleep.

Start a routine for older children by giving them 10 minutes' notice before bedtime to wind up whatever they are doing. The routine that follows should be a bath, into pyjamas, reading or looking at a picture book and then a quick cuddle before you say 'goodnight' and leave the room. The goal is to teach your child that bedtime is enjoyable, just as it is for us adults.

When to start a routine and get her into good bedtime habits depends on the age of the child. In the first few months premature babies should be treated according to their due date, not their birth date. Below are the key pointers for different ages and stages:

Newborns

o Newborn babies sleep for most of the day and periods of wakefulness can occur during both the day and night. A baby's stomach is very small and milk is easily digested, so she will wake often to be fed.

o In the first three months babies sleep between 10.5 and 18 hours per day, the average being 15–16 hours. Over the three-month period, the length of time spent asleep at night increases, while daytime sleep steadily decreases.

o By paying close attention parents begin to recognize their baby's sleep patterns and identify signs of sleepiness.

o A baby's only way of communicating is to cry for attention. Always respond to your newborn's crying; don't try to impose any sleeping routines by ignoring it before she is six weeks old.

o After about six weeks parents will observe a change in behaviour as their infant's circadian rhythms start to develop Your baby's longest sleep (around five hours) will now be at night.

o You can start to introduce certain practices that will encourage a good sleep routine later. When your baby is showing signs of sleepiness, always put her down in her cot to sleep. Reinforce emerging circadian rhythms by keeping the room dark at night.

o Follow the recommendations of child safety organizations when putting your baby to bed. Place your baby to sleep on her back with her face and head clear of blankets and other soft items.

○ Some babies may cry in the evening for a couple of hours and some can be inconsolable. This is often due to colic, a condition which generally clears at around three months. Whatever her age, if your baby is very distressed and in pain, be flexible with her routine.

Baby as room mate

Babies are recommended to sleep in their own cot in their parents' room for the first few months.

Infants: Three to 12 months

○ From three months to a year the total amount of sleep, on average, is 14.5–15 hours per 24-hour period. Infants typically sleep between 9 and 11 hours at night and will take two (occasionally three) naps per day.

○ Don't give your baby solids before about six months of age in the hope that it will make her sleep longer. It won't work.

○ This is an important stage for getting your child into good sleep habits. Try to ensure that she falls asleep in her own cot, not in your arms, your bed or elsewhere in the house. Don't encourage any sleep habits that require you to stay with your child until she falls asleep.

○ Keep the room dark and quiet and check that the temperature is not too hot.

Resisting routine

Not all children react in the same way to a bedtime routine. Some babies, by temperament, are less tractable than others and take longer to get into a routine.

○ In the second part of the first year children may experience separation anxiety. Fear of being separated from their parents can lead some children to become fretful and upset if they are alone. Babies who are clingy during the day and cry when their mother or father is out of sight are likely to experience problems at bedtime.

Toddlers: One to three years

○ From six months to three years, children tend to sleep between 10 and 14 hours per day. Although there will inevitably be occasional setbacks, a three year-old child should be in a regular and predictable night-time routine, sleeping all night without disturbance and waking refreshed and alert ready to face the day.

○ At some time in the second year the morning nap is dropped. There may need to be an adjustment to the sleep schedule when the nap goes.

○ Problems can arise in this period with the onset of growing independence, which is often expressed by contrariness and a tendency to say 'no'. Typical problems you might experience include a resistance to going to bed, refusing to settle and repeatedly getting out of bed to come downstairs as well as night-time waking.

○ Fears and fantasies are common in this age group as children's imagination develops. Some children become afraid of the dark, others worry about monsters under the bed and others worry about things they have seen on television or in picture books.

Pre-schoolers

○ Pre-schoolers typically have between 11 and 12 hours' sleep in total, and somewhere between the ages of three and five they will drop their afternoon nap.

○ Pre-schoolers are able to respond to discussions and understand the importance of rules. It becomes possible at this stage to explain why we need sleep. Reward charts can be added to the repertoire of possible solutions to sleeping problems.

○ During this period children are moving out of the family setting and into nursery school. They may be more tired after a morning at nursery and they may also experience new worries.

○ A child should sleep in the same environment every night: in a room that is cool, quiet and dark – and without a television.

School-age children

○ Once children start going to school they will often be very tired, especially in the first year. Sleep is very important now, and children who are chronically sleep-deprived may find that their academic performance is affected.

○ The discipline of waking up for school will reveal whether or not a child is getting enough sleep. If she is, she will wake easily in the morning and be fresh and alert.

○ There is a number of distractions that may push bedtime later and make it more difficult for the child to fall asleep. These include homework, after-school activities and television.

Why a bedtime routine is important

Security is about more than simply being loved. A child feels safe when she lives in an orderly and predictable world, where everything happens in line with her expectations.

The bedtime routine is a good example of predictability and routine, and you need to stick to it. Very few children sleep through every night: occasionally they wake up for medical or emotional reasons or because of changes in family circumstances or developmental changes. Be flexible in dealing with these occasional wakings, but remember that the basis of good sleeping habits is a predictable routine, so be sure to return to it as soon as you can. If your toddler is very persistent in coming to your room at night, the temptation to give in and let her sleep in your bed may be too great to resist. Try not to give in. Once this habit establishes itself it may prove very hard to break.

Keeping to the routine means setting limits that are consistent, communicated and enforced. Setting limits includes making sure that once your child has gone to sleep, she stays asleep. During the 'terrible twos', when children tend to start to assert themselves, maintaining firm boundaries is particularly important. This is when it is crucial that you are consistent and don't back down.

Be flexible and take into account changes in circumstances

The approaches outlined in this book will work for the majority of children, but all children and families are different and what works for some doesn't necessarily work for all.

When establishing good sleep habits the most important thing to learn is to use your understanding of your child to recognize her different cries. Never ignore a cry of pain, distress or hunger, but when a child is supposed to be asleep the cry that means 'I'm awake now and I would like some company' can safely be ignored. Your child will not come to any psychological harm if you disregard this type of crying.

There are certain predictable circumstances that will have an impact on the sleeping regime you have set up, though:

Teething, colds and minor ailments

In the early days, while you are trying to get your baby into a routine, teething and other minor ailments will often wake

Snuggle up

Encourage the use of a security object, such as a comfort blanket or stuffed animal, which will give your baby something to snuggle up to when you are not there.

her and may keep her awake at night. When these things happen you cannot rigidly stick to the routine. A baby who is in pain or distress needs to be soothed and comforted.

Separation anxiety

From seven or eight months onwards babies form strong attachments with one of their parents. If you are going to start training your child to sleep without you, start before this separation anxiety kicks in.

New baby, new house

Any significant change in family circumstances, such as a new sibling or moving to a new house, may cause toddlers to regress and could upset their sleep routine. Accept that your child will be disturbed in such situations, but stick to the broad principles of your routine where you can.

New bed, new mobility

At two or three years old children move to beds from cots and thus become more mobile. This is the period of midnight wandering and tantrums before bedtime.

New school, new routines

When a child starts school she may bring her worries home with her at the end of each day. Once she goes to bed, worries that have been buried amongst the activities of the day begin to surface and can keep her awake. Friendships, academic work and fears about the world in general are all likely sources of concern.

The longer a habit is established, the more difficult it is to change

The main problem parents have with children waking at night relates to what sleep experts call 'incorrect (or inappropriate) associations' with sleep. A baby gets used to being rocked to sleep, or falling asleep downstairs with her parents, so when she goes through a period of light sleep she needs those associations to help her go back to sleep.

It is possible to get a baby used to the idea of falling asleep in a cot, in a dark and quiet room, from the very beginning – even before the baby is able to sleep for any length at night-time.

Is this your ideal evening?

When you deviate from your established routine, think: 'Am I prepared to do this every evening or night?'

A word on co-sleeping

Many parents are reluctant to let their babies cry at all, so they choose to have their babies sleep with them. Many experts recommend this practice as one that gives babies a strong sense of security. In practical terms it means that a baby can be fed in bed with a minimum of disturbance. On the other hand, many paediatricians question the safety of bringing a very small baby into bed and instead suggest a compromise whereby the baby sleeps in the same room, close to the parent's bed, but not in it.

Sleeping with your baby is a personal choice and depends on what kind of sleepers the adults are. Parents who sleep badly – even without a baby or toddler in their bed – are advised not to start co-sleeping. Parents who do this should think ahead and ask themselves when and how they will get the baby to sleep alone in her own room. You don't have to be a psychoanalyst to see the psychological implication of fathers sleeping in their child's bed while the child sleeps with her mother!

When you have put your baby down she might cry a little as you leave the room. Don't go back immediately. Wait to see if she falls asleep without you being there. Remember that if she comes to associate falling asleep with you being with her, that's how she will always want to fall asleep, including when she wakes in the middle of the night.

There are strategies for dealing with sleep problems

Good sleep habits are not difficult to establish, but unfortunately neither are bad ones. The process of changing habits requires motivation, determination (and persistence) and consistency. All of the strategies outlined in this book rely on these qualities.

Motivation

Often parents see the need to change a child's sleeping habits as primarily for their own benefit. What they often fail to appreciate, though, is the importance to their child of regular and refreshing sleep. It is not good for a child to be waking regularly during the night and crying out for her parents.

Parents who are trying to deal with bad sleep habits need to be motivated, because it can be difficult to change them, and in the middle of the night when they are exhausted, the temptation to succumb to the quick fix and give in is very strong.

Determination

When habits have been established for several weeks, months or even years, it will take a great deal of determination to break them. The process of change requires steely determination, especially when you are confronted with a willful and assertive child.

Don't start the process of trying to break a habit unless you can carry it through to the end. Many of the strategies outlined in this book, such as controlled crying or holding the bedroom door closed to keep your child in her room, require parents to listen to their child's crying for longer and longer periods without going in to console her. This is not easy, but unless you are happy to let your child decide when she should go to bed or where she should sleep, you need to be determined to assert your authority and to set up the bedtime routine that is in her best interests. If you can't continue with a technique, don't start. Find another approach that works for you, but bear in mind that it might take longer.

Older children should not have televisions in their bedrooms. Research shows that children who do have screens in their rooms are more likely to be sleep-deprived. If your child tells you that everyone else in her class has a television in their bedroom, you need to stay strong and say 'no' to her.

Consistency

Once you decide on a course of action to solve your child's sleep problems, be consistent. It is important to do the same thing every night until the habit is broken. If you give in one day because you are tired and emotional, all the good work of the previous nights will be undermined. If you plan to change your child's sleeping habits and you know it won't be easy, make sure there are no other factors that will affect your resolve. Don't do it if you are going to be away for a time, if a holiday is approaching or if you have something important to do at work and need your sleep.

Shifting waking-up times naps and bedtimes will solve many problems

O Look at your child's overall pattern of sleep. Problems with infants' sleep can often be resolved by changing the scheduling of their sleep. Moving naps to earlier or later can influence the amount of night-time sleep and the times of going to bed and waking up.

O If a baby goes to bed too late or wakes up too early, it is usually best to adjust her waking time to create the sleep shift you want, since you cannot make a child sleep but you can rouse her when you want her to be up.

O Most planned changes meet more or less resistance depending on how long the habit has been established. The best approach is to make changes very slowly, usually by altering sleep or wake times in 15-minute intervals.

O Don't rely on catching up on sleep at the weekend as a way of dealing with too little sleep during the week: this will only perpetuate the sleep deprivation. Try to regulate weekday sleep times by shifting wake times and sleep times during the week.

Establish a sleep-friendly environment

○ Your child's bedroom should be dark, quiet and coolish.

○ Don't threaten to send a child to bed if she is naughty, or you will create a bad association with her bedroom. Bedtime needs to be a secure, loving time, not a punishment.

○ Even when a baby is not old enough to get into a routine, start to establish the right cues for sleep by darkening the room and keeping down any background noise.

○ If your baby needs additional help to drop off to sleep or to obscure background noise, use 'white noise'.

○ Use natural fabrics for bedding and sleepwear, as some babies cannot settle amongst synthetic materials. A raisingkids.co.uk member couldn't understand why her baby kept waking at night until she discovered her child was sensitive to polyester nightwear. Once she changed to 100 per cent cotton clothing, her baby slept better.

Finally, I hope this book has convinced you of the importance of sleep both for you and your baby. The ability to fall asleep and wake up refreshed is a gift from you to your child, as vital as the enjoyment of good food. Just as with good food, there are both physical and emotional health benefits to having a decent quality and quantity of sleep. Always remember that if you have got into bad habits and you and your child are sleep-deprived, there are things you can do to put it right. They may be difficult, but they don't take long and the benefits will be felt for years.

Resources

www.bbc.co.uk/parenting

The BBC website offers comprehensive advice and information for parents, with onward links to other useful sites.

www.parentlineplus.org.uk

Freephone: 0808 800 2222

Parentline Plus is a national charity that works for, and with, parents. It runs a free, confidential helpline for parents who need help and support which is staffed by trained volunteers 24 hours a day, 7 days a week.

www.raisingkids.co.uk

Website founded by the author of this book. It offers a wide range of information and advice to all parents, whatever the age of their children.

www.sleepforkids.org

An American website which is run by the National Sleep Foundation ad aims to highlight the importance of good sleep for health and well-being. There are sections for children, which include fun activities, and related sections for parents and teachers.

Books

Dr Marc Weissbluth: *Healthy Sleep Habits, Happy Child: A Step-by-step Programme for a Good Night's Sleep* (Vermillion)

Dr Marc Weissbluth founded the original Sleep Disorders Center at Chicago's Children's Memorial Hospital and is a prolific writer and broadcaster on the subject of children's sleep.

Dr Richard Ferber: *Solve Your Child's Sleep Problems: A Practical and Comprehensive Guide for Parents* (Dorling Kindersley)

This influential book on children's sleep problems is now over 20 years old. Dr Ferber is from the Center for Pediatric Sleep Disorders at the Children's Hospital in Boston, USA, and has given his name to a verb – 'to ferberise' – meaning to following his guidance in dealing with sleep problems.

Dr Tanya Byron: *Your Child Your Way: Create a Positive Parenting Pattern* (Michael Joseph)

Television parenting expert Dr Tanya Byron covers more topics than sleep in this book, but it is recommended here because the roots of many sleep issues are often to be found in the wider context of a parent's approach to rearing their child.